Sycamore Hill

A Search for God When Life Doesn't Make Sense

By Silouan Green

Published by Everon LLC
Copyright © 2015 by Everon LLC

ISBN-13: 978-0692483763
ISBN-10: 0692483764

Cover design and photography by Silouan Green

For quantity orders, please contact: Silouan@mac.com.

First print edition

For the broken, you are not alone

Acknowledgments

This book would not have been possible without the love of my family, especially my wife, Thecla, and our children: Isaac, Mary, Irene, Jude, Maximus, Georgia, Gabriel, and Josephine

To Albert Atkinson whose contribution helped make this possible.

To Trecia Phillips and Dana Runnebohm – Earth Movers.

A special thank you to all the indiegogo.com supporters, anonymous and public, who made the production and publishing of this book a reality.

I wrote this book for the men and women I've met this last decade struggling to overcome the many ways life can break us. This book is for you.

Most of all, I want to thank Jason. Without you asking me to write a book about our conversation, this would not have been written.

We have one life, may you live free.

Sycamore Hill by Silouan Green

Contents

Chapter 1:

All Roads

It had taken $45,000, a decent amount of money in 1985, but the old family property was exactly what he had remembered from his youth – quiet, remote, simple, and a long driveway. It even had a name, Sycamore Hill, which was identified by both an old hand-carved sign hanging at the entrance, and labeled on the official county survey map as Sycamore Hill.

The name, the trees, the long, winding driveway, David liked everything about the little oasis just a few miles from the college town of Bloomington, Indiana. Its 20 acres of land were bordered on two sides by Hoosier National Forest, and the remaining two sides, by a stream and frontage road. He would never have to worry about neighbors. Much of the land was covered with old growth hardwoods, and near the back edge bordering Hoosier National was an almost two-acre clearing containing an old cabin, an outhouse, and a woodshed. For generations the property had been used as a vacation retreat, but David would make it a home, a place where he could learn to live again.

That first day after signing the papers, handing over the check, and officially becoming the owner, he slept in the clearing under a canopy of stars and towering sycamore, dogwood, cedar, and maple trees. It was a symphony of nature, the night sky a celestial blanket that warmed his soul from the pain that had brought him to Sycamore Hill.

Would he finally find the peace for which he had been longing? Only time would tell, but he was off to a great start. This was the first night in memory where he had laid down to sleep and not been instantly suffocated by death – death that he saw in the faces of his family, shadows, all of whom were long gone – Mary, Mattie, Sam, and Sally Anne. *What a life we have ahead of us*, was a common thought of his when they were alive. Even when they were doing the most mundane things – eating supper, getting ready for church, working in the yard or cleaning out the garage – he could find joy in it all. But then they were taken away, suddenly, mercilessly, and in a flash there seemed no life ahead of him at all.

That first day had been over 30 years ago, and ever since David had been busy turning Sycamore Hill into a bastion of peace. The rundown cabin was now a model of simplicity, cleanliness, and utilitarian perfection. Each part of the structure was purposeful from the large iron door latch to the enormous hand water pump by the sink he used to draw water from the well.

The cabin was really one large room, with a sink and counter on the east wall, a desk and bookshelves on the south wall facing the front door, while a dresser and a bed that doubled as a couch for visitors rested against the west wall. In the middle of the room was a large cast iron stove he used for heating and cooking and next to it sat a wooden rocking chair for sitting and reading. There was only one picture, a portrait of his family that had taken him years after arriving to hang. The idea of looking at the picture was too much to bear in the beginning, but as he healed it took its place above his bed, watching over him as he slept. There was a cross hanging on the wall over his desk, a simple wood desk he had made from lumber on the property. Upon the desk were his journal, a pen, and his well-worn Bible. A Bible he cried in, a Bible he had thrown against the wall. But like David, it had survived.

The sole electrical device in the cabin, his one luxury, was a small refrigerator next to the sink. He had tried to live without it those first few years, but the constant need for fresh food just became a distraction, so he took advantage of the power line that had been run onto the property by its previous owners, and wired a refrigerator. It came in handy for serving guests drinks and a snack, usually sweet pickles he had made from the cucumbers he grew in his garden. Other than the refrigerator and some basic power tools he used for construction and maintenance on the property, he was electricity free.

And there were guests, hundreds, if not thousands of them over the years. It had been completely unexpected to David. While he had never thought of himself as a hermit, he had arrived at Sycamore Hill looking for isolation and peace. The few places in nearby Bloomington he visited didn't take long to recognize him as a regular. Conversations would invariably come up from the many students and locals he met at his two main destinations, Blooming Foods and the Ace Hardware store, usually asking about his seclusion and Sycamore Hill. It did not take long for people to see him as a sort of guru and begin to lean on him for advice. Most visits to town would end with him telling a new friend, "Stop by if you ever need to talk." David would write down directions on a piece of paper, smile, and say, "Hope to see you soon." A few days later they would usually come, stay a few hours, and more often than not, leave with their life changed. As word got out, David's reputation spread, and most days someone would make the long trek up the drive to the clearing and David's cabin.

Today, like most, David woke up early, a little after 5 am. His first order of business was tending to the animals: chickens, goats, and a milk cow. With that finished, he would work in the garden and yard and then wash up by pumping water into the kitchen sink. He always made sure to shave, a habit he had begun when he started dating Mary. She liked him clean-shaven; he had continued the ritual upon moving to Sycamore Hill. Every morning it was a bridge to the memory of those he loved – his wife who loved his clean-shaven face, his children who liked to play with his shaving soap and watch every stroke of his blade.

Along with the memories, splashing that cold well water on his face after a little manual labor was invigorating. Wide awake as he dried his face looking out the window over the sink into the forest surrounding his home, he was ready to face the day and live.

After chores, he would usually make a simple breakfast of oatmeal and coffee and then sit on his porch where he would read his Bible and pray. When his reading and prayers were over, he would do more work in the yard or continue reading as he waited for them to come. It might be the existential crisis of a young college student on their own for the first time and making bad decisions. For others, it was a mid-life crisis, or a death, or some unexplainable tragedy. It could be a grieving veteran or a woman whose youth had been ripped away and who had never been able to find peace. He would see them coming up the drive, and he would start to pray. Silently, he would look up into the sky, smell the trees, and open his heart to the soul making his or her way to him for hope and answers. Answers they would receive, and after many years of this simple life – little more than chores and talking – David had found that God rarely let him down. He would pray, and somehow, the words would come and he would know exactly what these pilgrims needed to hear.

Today was a day that David would definitely need some divine help in answering questions. Jason and Zoe were coming, although Zoe didn't know it yet. Jason had made up his mind to come a few days earlier. He did not have many other options left and when he heard about David from a friend he thought a journey to Sycamore Hill might just be his last and best chance for hope. Zoe had cut herself again the night before and lost blood. Waking in the ER to find that she was alive thanks to a friend who had stopped by her apartment to find her unconscious in bed with barely a pulse, Zoe's rescue felt like a dark burden and she wished she had been left to die. She was tired of fighting and tired of living for what little meaning she could find in the pain. Leaving the hospital after she refused to stay and be monitored, her agenda for the day had been to enjoy a couple of the things she loved, mountain biking and a drink from her favorite coffee shop, the Runciple Spoon. After this, she was going to go home, take some pills, down a glass of her favorite Merlot, slide into a warm bath, and slit her wrists. She hoped to just fade away. She would make sure the door was locked this time so no one could stop by and interrupt her plans.

Fortunately for Zoe, there would be other plans on the table for her today.

Not today Zoe, not today. You will not enter the darkness. Today you have people to meet, and soon you will all be together on Sycamore Hill where hope is found.

Chapter 2:

Dirty Hippies

It wasn't the proverbial VW mini-bus, but Jason's dark blue Ford Econoline van was still built for the road. Although it was over a decade old and carried almost 175,000 miles, these warhorses were made for durability and this steed had many more years and miles left to roam. Jason had removed all the rear seats and turned the space into a mini-camper with a bed, table, and even a chair. He had spent the last three months fixing it up, starting with the mechanical necessities (i.e., the kind of stuff that leaves you stranded), brakes, tires, belts, hoses, etc., and then moving on to the interior and the comforts he would need for life on the road. It was almost ready and in a few days he hoped the trip could begin. Before he left though, he had a couple of loose ends to tie up and one very important mission to complete here in Bloomington. Jason intended to find a man he had heard about from friends who had also been looking for answers, the mythical man in the woods, David. He hoped David could help him make sense of the dark thoughts consuming him. Jason needed hope that he could overcome them or the final destination of his road trip would just be more misery.

Some said David was a hermit, others a priest, others a hippie living alone in the woods. Universally though, no one had anything bad to say about him, and most had incredible stories about the most broken people visiting David and returning transformed. Jason was not one to believe in gurus, but when the demons of his military service as a US Marine in Iraq finally had made it impossible for him to continue in school at Indiana University where he had been studying business at the Kelley School, he began searching for someone who could help him make sense of the senselessness he had seen in the sandbox. Living in Bloomington, that journey led him to David.

David had been easy to spot about a week earlier when Jason met him while shopping at Blooming Foods. He had learned that David shopped there so, although his food budget did not really allow for organic shopping, he had made a habit of stopping by the past couple weeks looking for him. Jason had received a pretty specific description of David from a friend – he was in his sixties but looked 10 years younger, tanned, trim, clean-shaven with a touch of gray in his short cut hair. His eyes were a dark hazel, and a Roman nose contributed to his strong bearing. He wore well-worn leather boots and clothes that had been patched many times, yet he did not look like a hermit or a bum; no, there was something neat and orderly about him. The patches were done cleanly and expertly, the boots, while old, seemed well taken care of and were of the highest quality. He was a man of purpose and no nonsense who only used what he needed.

More than any one aspect of his physical

appearance, David shined friendliness. He smiled at everyone. He stopped to warmly watch children walk by. He spoke to anyone who said hello and walked intentionally while never in much of a hurry. If peace could be a person it was David. It made it easy for Jason to approach him.

"Uh, excuse me, sir," Jason sputtered as he walked down the produce aisle where David was examining mangos. David returned a smile, then fixed his eyes on Jason's.

"Can I help you?" David returned Jason's greeting.

"Yes, sir," Jason answered, then continued, "Sorry to bother you, but are you David, that man in the woods people talk about?"

"Yes, I am," David answered. Jason looked like a man on a mission so David was not surprised at Jason's bluntness and had met many young men like him before. "What can I do for you?" David had no problem obliging Jason but got right to the point; he had shopping to do.

"Well, I'd like to speak with you one day soon if you have time," Jason said. "I'm leaving Bloomington and thought I'd try to talk to you before I left," Jason explained.

"You can stop by anytime from sunup to sundown," David replied. "Here, let me draw you a map. I'm usually home except for Mondays when I run errands. What is your name by the way?"

"Jason," he answered.

"Well, here you are, Jason." David handed him the map. "I hope to see you soon."

Early on a Tuesday morning, a little over a week after their first meeting at Blooming Foods, Jason was on his way to see David. First things first though; he felt like splurging a little and was going to stop by a Bloomington landmark, the Runciple Spoon, for a Dirty Hippie and a big bowl of lentil soup. Dirty hippie you wonder? Well, it was a taste explosion of steamed milk, Chai tea, and espresso, and the Runciple Spoon made the best one on the planet.

Little did Jason know that at that very moment fate was walking his way, the kind you don't see coming. Her name was Zoe, a former student on a very different journey than his. She was walking from her apartment down Second Street to visit the Runciple Spoon for the same Dirty Hippie. Her plans for the day were very deliberate with a to-do list. Her first checked box had been a mountain bike ride around Griffey Lake, which she had completed in record time and rode herself to exhaustion. Second on her list of things to do was the Runciple Spoon. It was a day she planned on ending with a warm bath and a razor blade. Surprisingly, the decision to end it all had brought Zoe a numb peace and the walk to the Spoon after her bike ride was actually pleasant. As she approached the familiar building and its Japanese manicured front walkway, life actually seemed calm – at least what life she had left.

Jason and Zoe arrived almost simultaneously; Zoe approached the Runciple Spoon first followed by Jason, who paid the respect of reaching ahead and opening the Spoon's door for her. Jason still possessed the athletic body he had developed in the Marines, and Zoe spent most of her time on a mountain bike, so the glances they passed due to Jason's politeness on most other days might have led to immediate flirting, but today they were both serious and on a mission. Jason was thinking about what he would be asking and revealing to David, while Zoe was focused on her day's agenda and rendezvous with death.

Then Zoe ordered a Dirty Hippie and Jason couldn't help but comment:

"A Dirty Hippie?" he questioned with a smile and she turned to face him. "Excellent choice, that's what I was going to order."

"Yes it is," she said simply.

Jason immediately liked the sprite young lady in a well-worn sundress, and since he was already splurging on himself thought that he would treat the fellow Dirty Hippie lover.

"Well, I'm splurging today and leaving town soon, so let me pay for yours," he offered.

"Are you sure?" she questioned, not used to

spontaneous generosity. None of her friends had much money, especially for buying others four-dollar specialty drinks. But more importantly, she was broke and his kindness seemed genuine rather than manipulative. She had met more than a few fraternity boys who liked to throw money around. But not Jason, he didn't come across like that. There was something familiar about him.

"Yes, I'm sure," he replied and leaned over the counter where he ordered two Dirty Hippies and paid for them both. At the end of the counter they waited for their drinks and got further acquainted.

"I'm Jason," he said, introducing himself and extending his hand.

"Zoe," she replied as she returned his handshake. It was then she was sure. It was him. *I can't believe it's him.* She wanted to thank him, but couldn't. She couldn't let him know she knew. She didn't want to explain and be known as "that girl." Yet, she couldn't leave with just an introduction. So surprisingly, especially for Zoe, the shy girl with an end of the day death wish and heart-stopping recognition of Jason continued the conversation. "So, you are leaving town? Where to?"

"I'm not completely sure," he explained with a smile and a shrug. "I just know that I need to hit the road and figure some things out. I have money saved from when I was in the Marines and I'm going to drive out west. I outfitted an old van for camping and I plan on leaving in a week or two. Just have a few more things to do before I leave."

"Well, that sounds like an adventure. You were in the Marines?" None of Zoe's friends had served and a Marine on a trip was an exotic thing to her.

"Yes, ma'am, I was in the Marines." He liked the way ma'am and Marines sounded together. "That was a while ago though," Jason paused then continued, "To be honest, I just can't stay here any longer."

"Why is that?" she asked. Things were quickly getting serious. Their drinks arrived and then they very naturally sat down together in a warm wooden booth as Jason answered her question.

"I need to find someplace else. Somewhere I belong. I went to college right after I got out of the Marines and too many things stayed with me. I just can't do the college thing now."

"I know what you mean." Zoe understood. "My last semester was tough. It dragged on and I got to the point that I wasn't even going to class. I would get up most mornings intending to go, but I would usually just ride through campus on my mountain bike and end up in the woods. That's about all I did, bike, hike, and work at the bagel shop. I think I'm done with school, too." Her voice trailed off as she finished the last sentence. She was finished with more than school.

"So where are you going then if you're done with school?" Jason asked, figuring she had travel plans, too.

"Going?" She paused, caught off guard at the reasonable question. One would assume if you were dropping out of school you'd be leaving a college town. Of course, the only place she planned on going was into the darkness later that night. "Well, I hadn't planned on going anywhere right now. I don't really have anywhere to go."

"C'mon now," Jason encouraged her. "Lots of places to go, even right here around Bloomington. Heck, I'm going to see some hermit today."

"You mean that man who lives out near Hoosier National? I've heard about him." Her eyes perked up and she leaned closer to Jason, genuinely interested.

"The one and only. His name is David. I met him last week at Blooming Foods and he was surprisingly normal. Actually, he was warm, if someone could be warm." Jason smiled at his peculiar description. "I had just stopped by here on my way to see him."

"Really?" Zoe asked taken aback.

"Really," Jason replied, and then in a moment of inspiration, fate struck again. "You want to come with me, it'll be a little adventure."

"Well," she paused for a second as if she needed to think about it, but she had instantly known the answer.

Considering how wild it was to her that she had finally met HIM, the guy, the idea of meeting the mythical David was too much for even her in her suicidal state to resist. "Sure, let's go." And that is how they arrived at David's together.

"Great." Jason was happy. "We can finish our Dirty Hippies along the way. It'll take us about 15 minutes to get there, according to the map."

"Map?" With the advent of smartphones and GPS, one hardly heard the word map anymore.

"He actually drew me a map," Jason explained. "Said he felt better having people find his place with a map than staring at a phone. Kind of cool actually, it's like a little piece of art." Jason showed her the map David had carefully drawn to scale along with the landmarks they'd come across along the way – a church, railroad tracks, a field of sunflowers, and an old grain elevator.

"That is something," she commented looking at the map. "With a map like that, I wonder what his home will look like. What does it say there, Sycamore Hill?" Zoe actually seemed enthused. When was the last time she had been excited about anything? She couldn't remember.

They left as one, two pilgrims with a singular destination, Sycamore Hill. The rest of the trip was small talk about school, studies, love of mountain biking, and other mundane information common to college students or young former college students. Then, just as suddenly as they had met, they arrived at Sycamore Hill. There was a chain across the driveway and underneath the finely carved sign that read *Welcome to Sycamore Hill* was a smaller sign, *Please park here, no cars.* Jason parked his van next to an old pickup truck and together they began the walk up to Sycamore Hill where David was waiting.

Chapter 3:

Sycamore Hill

It had once been a gravel-lined driveway, unkempt for most of the year when Sycamore Hill was a vacation retreat. David had quickly turned the drive into an exquisitely manicured nature path. About three feet wide, it worked its way from the parking area by the road through trees and up the grade to the summit of Sycamore Hill. David kept the pebbles lining the walkway neat and tidy, tending to the washed out spots after storms and those kicked out of place by the many visitors.

Jason and Zoe were slowly making their way up the quarter-mile path. It was hard to move fast; everything around them was a wonderland and a feast for the eyes. There were bird feeders swarmed by birds of all colors, salt licks worn to nubs by armies of deer, flowers everywhere, a small shallow pond stocked with large orange fish, many wooden seats and benches and what looked like little grottos scattered throughout the surrounding woods. Was this place real? They had not been the first, nor would they be the last visitors to be overwhelmed by this magical world hidden only a few minutes east of town.

For the first few steps neither Jason nor Zoe spoke, but as they ventured further into the woods and up towards David's cabin their thoughts began to explode.

"Just look at all of that. I wonder if he did all of this himself?" Zoe exclaimed, not believing the variety of life surrounding them as far back into the woods as one could see.

"Seriously," Jason agreed. "Look at all the animals, the woodwork, those little grottos, everything is neat and clean. I hope he doesn't put us to work; no way he does this all himself." No way, but yes, there was a way. This was David's life and everything surrounding them had been created with a plan and a purpose. Of course, he always was willing to accept a hand from visitors who wanted to pitch in and help. Work can be better than therapy and it was often where the most healing conversations took place.

Near the end of the trail it rose steeply and one could look ahead and see where the trees opened up into a clearing. As they crested the hill there was David. He was working in his garden and there was even more wildlife. Bright red cardinals danced in a birdbath in the middle of the garden next to where David was digging in a flowerbed. Before they could make their way across the clearing to David, he was already heading toward them.

"Well, hello there, Jason," he called, extending his hand, remembering Jason's name. "Who is your friend?" David asked about Zoe as they shook hands. It was a friendly question asked with an inflection that said, *I'm glad she's here.*

Zoe smiled and Jason answered, "Zoe. We just met at the Runciple Spoon."

"The Runciple Spoon? They have some of the best

coffee and breakfast food in Bloomington," David affirmed.

"Yes, sir, they sure do," Jason concurred. "Can't usually afford it but today I really wanted to get myself a Dirty Hippie and that is where I met Zoe. She's a Dirty Hippie fan, too."

"Dirty Hippie? Well, then, we'll all be great friends." David turned toward Zoe then back at Jason. "I love Dirty Hippies. I guess I'd better, considering most people around here think I'm some dirty hippie living in the woods." David laughed. "Let's sit down. I have some chairs on the porch and I'll get you both some tea I've been chilling in the refrigerator. Oh, and I'll bring some sweet pickles, I make them myself." Zoe's eyes arched; she'd never had homemade sweet pickles and David continued, "We can talk and then maybe later you'll have time to explore the woods. And Jason, you don't have to call me 'sir.'"

"You got it. I learned 'sir' very well in the Marines," Jason said with a grin.

"I bet you did," David acknowledged.

They walked up to the porch together. Jason and Zoe sat down in a couple of wooden rockers while David went inside for the tea. He came back a few minutes later with a tray holding a pitcher of tea, some glasses filled with ice, and a plate piled with sliced sweet pickles. In his absence, Zoe and Jason had just sat there silently, continuing to breathe in David's little paradise.

"Here you go, sun tea and sweet pickles. Nature's best." David filled the glasses and handed them to Jason and Zoe along with the plate of pickles.

"Thanks," said Jason.

"Thank you," followed Zoe.

"So what brings you all here today?" David asked. He had learned it was usually best to get right to the point. If someone had made it this far, they wanted to talk. Jason would do most of the talking today as Zoe hadn't really been prepared for conversation, but she listened to every word and most of what was said would strike her soul deeply.

"I guess it's me," Jason started, and then paused for a second to take a drink of tea. "I've never quite made it home, so to speak, since I returned from Iraq with the Marines. I thought going to school would help but I just couldn't seem to fit in, or concentrate much. I dropped out after last semester, and most of the last few months I've been fixing up a van to hit the road. I thought maybe I'd find something there. I heard about you from some friends, so I thought I'd try to talk to you before I left." Jason was so worn out from life; he couldn't help but be succinctly honest.

David looked over at Zoe to see if she had

something to say but she just sat still, listening. She seemed to be enjoying the sweet pickles. So David started asking questions.

"What do you mean by, 'I've never made it home?'" David asked, honing in on Jason's words.

"Well, I guess I mean I'm still there. Very few moments go by when I'm not thinking about Iraq. You know, friends who didn't make it back and other things."

"You mean people you killed?" David took a leap.

"Yes," Jason answered and lowered his eyes.

"You are not alone, Jason," David assured him. "Many others like you have come walking up that trail. War is a heavy burden and can leave holes in one's soul that they don't think can ever be repaired."

"Hole is right," Jason agreed.

"And it is more than that really," David continued. "If you are like the others, you saw things so evil, and partook in horrific things, that your entire sense of right and wrong has been scrambled. Am I right?"

"Yes," Jason kept agreeing but couldn't look David in the eye.

"How about the guilt?" David leaned closer. "What is your guilt?"

"What do you mean?" Jason asked, but he knew.

"You know what I mean," David prodded him. "Soul-crushing guilt. Friends who died, maybe you even felt responsible for their death. Children you had to kill in battle because they had a gun pointed at you, or a bomb in their hand. Others that you killed but were wrong about what they were doing, and you feel their innocence on your hands."

Jason lowered his head further. He could not speak. He knew the guilt. He had seen it all. To this day, he could not get out of the blood. Zoe, who before leaving to get coffee had not even dreamed of visiting David or meeting Jason was starting to get a little overwhelmed by it all, and protective of her new, yet very well known to her, friend Jason.

"Blood, children, evil," Zoe stated with a slight hint of indignation and a stern look at David. "Why bring all that up? He came here for help." Her nature was to protect and she wanted to put an arm around Jason and tell David he was wrong. Jason quickly set the record straight though.

"No, no, he's right." Jason looked over at Zoe. "That's why I'm here. The faces, the guilt. Every night the faces, every day the weight on my chest and the memories of my friends. It's hard to bear." Zoe remained quiet yet still cast a distrusting glance at David. He better know what he was doing.

"You are not alone, Jason. We can only bear so much guilt and despair until we start sliding down a black hole where we think we are completely alone." David's hand was on Jason's leg and he spoke warmly with kind assuredness. "Of course, we are not really alone. Death and despair and anguish are as old as life itself. The questions we ask that we can't find answers to have been asked before. We tend to forget that our pain is not much different than everyone else's, we are all human."

"Great, so I'm not alone." Jason now looked up with sarcasm etched across his face. "What good does that realization do for me?"

David smiled, but not too wide. "It just means what it means, you are not alone."

It felt like an anti-climactic answer to an emotional conversation, and everyone sat silent for a moment. Yet, it was true. They were not alone, and it was pain that had brought them all together.

"I guess that makes sense. That's probably why I came here," Jason said with a shrug. "I wasn't expecting any answers. I figured I had thought everything through and there were no answers. I was just tired of being alone with it all." He stopped for a second to think and then affirmed David, "You are right. It does mean something to be here together. I never thought I could begin to talk about this stuff, especially with people who hadn't seen the same things I saw and did over there." This thinking had only led him to isolation, and isolation was not a kind partner to the fear, shame, and guilt he had been carrying about his time in Iraq.

"We are the only ones who walk in our own shoes, Jason," David explained. "It is not about who has walked in our shoes, it's about who will walk alongside us moving forward. You will never fully fill shoes of regret, but you already have two people here willing to walk with you and find a new path." David looked over at Zoe and smiled at her. He liked to end sentences with warm smiles, even hard to hear sentences.

Jason looked up at Zoe and then at David and marveled at how his entire life looked different in the company of these two new friends. Different, but could he ever really get rid of the burden? Could he ever forgive all that needed forgiven? Could he be forgiven? Could he ever stop cursing God? He wanted so badly to believe there was a reason for all the hell he had experienced.

They were quiet again. David decided to let them off the hook. He wanted them to chew a little on what had just been said, and he figured they would need to come back, probably more than once, especially Zoe. He could sense that in some ways, her pain ran deeper than Jason's and would take much more time to heal.

"I'll tell you two what. Let's finish this conversation later. I have some chores to do, and you need to get this young lady back home. But before you do, why don't you take a walk on one of my trails while I feed the chickens,"

David suggested as he put his hand on Zoe's shoulder. Surprisingly, Zoe did not recoil. She usually didn't like men touching her, especially men she had just met.

As David walked away to tend to his chores, Jason headed toward the trail head just a few yards from where they had been talking. Zoe came along, and although they didn't know it yet, they were headed toward the stream that crossed David's property. It was called Pete's Run and had been bubbling up from a spring about a mile away as long as anyone could remember.

Walking along the trail through the woods, they got a closer view of the wonders they had seen walking up the drive to David's home. There were bird feeders everywhere. Most were hand-carved and occupied by at least one perching bird. As the stream came into view, they could see a little bench on the bank made from two tree stumps and a piece of lumber nailed across the top of them. They hadn't talked walking down and both were hypnotized by the sounds of birds echoing in the woods and the hum of the stream growing louder as they drew near. Sitting down on the bench, Zoe couldn't help but describe it all.

"It's like a paradise or a holy place. Funny, I've never stepped foot in a church once in my life." Zoe smiled at the anecdote and meant it. Something was special about Sycamore Hill.

"I know," Jason agreed, he could feel something

too. "Did you notice how those birds didn't fly away even though a couple of those feeders were only a few feet from us when we walked by?"

"I did. I've never been that close to birds when they were talking to each other. I wished I could have joined them." She shuffled her bottom to get more comfortable on the wood seat.

"Yeah, this is the kind of place you don't want to leave," Jason said under the low hum of the creek. "I can understand why David has been here so long and kept building it up. I bet he loses track of time caring for this place."

"Look at the stream," Zoe said, as they both turned their eyes to the water, "It's so clean and clear."

"Although it's probably filled with bacteria," Jason added sarcastically, yet good-naturedly.

"Bacteria, no way! Watch, I'll drink some right now." Zoe darted from the bench, walked into the stream with her shoes on, cupped her hands, and scooped up a handful of water and drank. It was pure, clean, and clear. "That was great! Try some, Jason," she invited him as water dripped off her chin.

Jason obliged. He walked into the water for his own drink and concurred with Zoe.

"Man, that was awesome." They both then bent over and drank until their bellies were bloated. It was a grand feeling.

"I guess we better be going," Zoe suggested, thinking about where they were and why they had come. "David is probably waiting for us." Drinking water had brought them close together, and in that moment, she had gotten uncomfortable. It was the isolation in the woods and close proximity to a man. Even though she had recognized Jason, they had just met and she wasn't entirely comfortable around him yet. More than anything, she didn't want to ruin this moment with a feeling of being uncomfortable. If she left now, the peace and joy are what she'd bring with her.

"Sure," Jason agreed. He wasn't ready to go, but knew he needed to go, so much to do before he left on his trip.

With that they turned and walked out of the stream up the trail to David's. When they arrived, David had finished his chores and was sitting on the porch waiting for them.

"Looks like you found the stream," David commented.

"How could we miss it?" Jason followed with a grin.

"It was incredible. What a great place to walk down to," Zoe said thankfully.

Neither walked up on the porch; they stood in front

of the cabin and Jason said goodbye first.

"We better get going," Jason stated. "Thank you so much for the talk, and the tea."

"Yes, thank you," Zoe concurred.

"It was my pleasure. Sycamore Hill seems to come to life whenever I have visitors." David had only spoke half the truth. It was always alive, but when visitors came, it was as if the animals and the forest knew it was time to help David in his mission to help others.

"Oh, we'll be back," Jason replied, and he meant it. He had found a glimpse of peace here at Sycamore Hill and he wanted more of it, plus more of David's wisdom and comfort.

"If you can, come back tomorrow afternoon and we will talk some more," David invited. "I make my own maple syrup from trees here on the land and I'll have a little midday snack of griddlecakes and syrup waiting for you!" David clapped his hands together. Griddlecakes and real maple syrup always got him excited. His mother had made him his first batch when he was three and he had been hooked ever since. She insisted on real maple syrup, and over the years, there were few things he liked better. Plus, it reminded him of the family breakfasts that had always brought him joy.

"Can't pass that up, can we?" Jason agreed and looked at Zoe for confirmation that she gave with a nod. "I guess we'll see you then, SIR," Jason said with a wink, which caused David to immediately grin. As they turned to walk away, David leaned toward Zoe where he whispered in her ear, out of earshot of Jason. Once they had waved goodbye and were down the trail out of site from the house, Jason couldn't help but ask what David had said.

"What did he say to you back there?" Jason queried.

"That's none of your business," Zoe teased good-naturedly, trying to avoid the question.

"C'mon, what did he say?" Jason prodded.

"He said, 'save that bottle of Merlot for later, we'll make a toast with it someday.'" Zoe gave in with a brave face and the same masked smile, but now she felt like crying and was trying hard not to show it.

"Huh? Merlot? What does that mean?" Jason commented on the seemingly strange remark.

"A lot. It means a lot," Zoe answered in a tone that said *don't ask why*, then followed with a nice warning, "Now keep quiet and maybe you can toast with us." She then kicked a few stones at Jason and ran ahead. It was playful, but it was meant to definitely conclude the line of questioning. Jason was smart enough to recognize it was time to be patient and oblige.

"Save the Merlot for later." Those words sure did mean a lot to Zoe. She would take a warm bath that night but she wouldn't cut her wrists. In fact, she would go to an

Ultimate Frisbee practice that she had planned on skipping, but now felt eager to attend and run till she dropped. Her friend Carrie might even bring her dog Veda. Veda, a rambunctious border collie, always seemed to put her in a good mood. And after that, about all she could envision was sitting in the warm suds of her bubble bath and contemplate her return trip to Sycamore Hill and what she would ask David. The question she wanted to ask but probably wouldn't, *how had he known what her plans were?*

After dropping off Zoe, Jason returned to his apartment and lay in bed, trying to understand where this was all going. He liked David a lot, but how was any of this psychobabble going to help. He stared at the picture of himself and Jimmy in Iraq, Jimmy who had been turned to pink mist by an IED. How could he ever bear that? How could 'talk' ease that pain? Yet, he knew that Sycamore Hill and David's counseling were working their way into dark places he had been afraid to reveal to anyone. Places that screamed at him, "You are a monster, no one will understand. No one will forgive what you did." In spite of these voices and the despair and cynicism that accompanied them, like Zoe, he couldn't wait to go back to Sycamore Hill.

Chapter 4:

Knees

"No, I'm not okay. Mind your own business," David shouted with a grumble at the woman who had just put a soft hand on his shoulder and asked how he was doing. He had been living at Sycamore Hill a few weeks and was standing in the cereal aisle of Blooming Foods, perfectly still, with tears running down his face. His hand was frozen on a box of Cheerios. They had been his children's favorite.

David turned to face her. She was white-haired in her late sixties and David's shout had shocked her. Now looking at her flushed face, he was slapped back to the reality of his present rudeness. *What is happening to me? I wanted to escape this,* he quickly thought to himself then apologized to the woman, "I'm sorry. I am very sorry." The woman walked away without a response, more than a little unsettled. David took a few steps after her to try and explain, then stopped. He just wanted to get back to the property and work.

He had been spending his time at Sycamore Hill on the many chores and upkeep that needed to be done, and which helped him get through those first days. Whether it was clearing the land or repairing the cabin, the hard work helped him focus and kept his mind occupied. He did his best to work all day until exhaustion and would only try to sleep when it seemed he had expended every bit of energy he possessed. The first night the exhaustion worked; he did in fact get some rest. But soon the routine caught up with him and the demons returned. Night was a battle he couldn't seem to win. No matter how exhausted he became before climbing into his sleeping bag, the moment he closed his eyes they came.

"No! Don't go. Don't go!!!" David was screaming. He was in a dark room with a window looking out onto that day. He was locked in the prison by his dreams and nobody could hear his cries. He was helpless, and guilty. His entire life, an eternity in hell, he would offer it all to change that one day.

"Sure you don't want to come with us, David?" his wife Mary asked with a smile that grew into a frustrated grimace as David kept refusing, eager to stay home and work out.

"Daddy, you can work out later," the children pleaded, tugging on his shirt.

"David, you've been traveling all week. The kids want to be with you." Mary's hands were on her hips and her head was crooked slightly to the left; she could never understand men, much less David.

"Just go ahead, I'll meet you later. I need to work out and take a shower," David tried to explain while Mary and the kids kept staring, highly annoyed at his stubborn nature. "C'mon on, just let me get this done," he spoke as he thought to himself, *seriously, just go.*

Exasperated, they finally gave up and walked out the front door. As they drove away, David began screaming from the black room. As always, it was an unanswered scream of terror.

"Stop, come back. Come back. Wait for me, I'll come with you. I'm sorry. Stop!!!!"

They never stopped and they never came back. The dream always ended the same way, just like that fateful day. Every one of them dead, hit head on as Mary turned to reprimand a loud child and inadvertently swerved into a tractor-trailer. David blamed himself. 100% blamed himself. *If I'd been there, they would all be alive.*

It was a blame he shared though. God was to blame. Where was God? David had grown up listening to preachers who extolled the virtues of "God is always in control." Really? He let my family die. He let my little girl suffer. If that is God in control I want no part of God. He can suck any lessons I was supposed to learn thanks to their suffering. Mattie, their oldest, had lived for a few tortured minutes. Just long enough to see the blood and death surrounding her. Then she died alone. The truck driver told the police he could hear her screaming, begging for help, and for her father.

"Daddy, Daddy! Help us, Daddy! Where are you?"

Darkness. Despair. Guilt. It was the same dream every time.

Covered in sweat, David rose from his sleeping bag and walked across the rough floor of the cabin toward the front door. Along the way, in the dark, he kicked the Bible he had thrown across the room before trying to sleep. He lit his Coleman lantern so he would not stumble across something else and then picked up the Bible only to slam it back down on his desk. The Bible came to rest with an open page and David saw the words of Christ in red, "My God, My God, why hast thou forsaken me." He paused for a minute. The words jolted him, but before he could consider why, the words and images of his dream began to swarm his brain.

"Come with us, David."

"Daddy, please."

"Do you have to work out now?"

"Daddy, help me. Where are you?"

And then there were more screams, blood, destruction, and a broken, dying girl screaming for her father, as the rest of her family lay crushed around her in a soup of metal and plastic.

David ran out his front door into the night. It was after midnight and the sky was clear, glittering stars hung in every direction. To most it would have been beautiful. To

David, it was an insult.

"You!!!!" he screamed, staring a hole into the sky. "You!!!! Where are you?" He ran around the yard, throwing lumber and tools from the projects he had been working on. It took a few minutes, but he did not stop until everything was torn apart and strewn across the grounds. Empty, he fell to his knees and began to weep in the middle of the mess. Despairing words and unanswerable questions drove corkscrews through his head.

There is no God. There is no sense to all of this. My family is worm food as I will be someday. It was all my fault. I deserve to be dead. God is a joke. The Bible is a myth written by sheepherders and I'm mad at a spaghetti monster in the sky . . . and on he went.

Yet those words kept being interrupted by the image of Christ suffering on the cross, looking up at God and crying out with the same anguish and desperation as David felt now, "My God, My God, why hast thou forsaken me?" The words resonated; somehow David knew that Christ understood his anger and despair.

David cried himself out and the words of hate began to recede. He slumped into the grass. He wanted to stay mad, but it was hard because he didn't feel alone anymore. Looking up at the stars, instead of invoking anger at the God who had created them, it made him feel closer to his compatriot in despair, the carpenter on a cross wondering who was going to save him from crucifixion and a lonely bitter death.

David dozed off with these thoughts and woke a few hours later covered in dew. The sky was a deeper shade of black, which made the stars even more brilliant. Wiping the moisture off his arms, he returned to the cabin. Thinking that he would not be able to sleep, he decided to make some coffee. Stoking the fire still smoldering in his stove, the glow of the open door focused his attention on the Bible he had thrown earlier and which was still laying open on his table. He walked over to pick it up, sat down, and then opened it to those words that had jolted him earlier, "My God, My God, why hast thou forsaken me."

Christ knew exactly how he felt – despairing, angry, hopeless, in pain, and feeling alone. And for that very reason, David knew he was not alone. At that moment, under the stars in this simple cabin, he had never felt less alone, even when his family was alive. And if he wasn't alone, a sort of brother-in-despair with the Creator's son, well then neither was his family. They were under the stars together. He cried and he smiled, and he took the coffee percolator off the stove without taking a drink. He could sleep now.

David woke up early the next day feeling rested; if he'd had a mirror he might have seen that he looked a decade younger, yet he had only slept a few hours. He was incredibly alive and this new energy made him manic to work. He pulled on his boots and walked outside more determined than ever to build Sycamore Hill into something that mattered, if only to him, God, and his family. But that was enough.

Little did David know that it wouldn't just be for him. He was also building it for many other people staring into the same abyss of doubt, despair, and hopelessness from which he had climbed. Soon they would come and Sycamore Hill would be ready.

Chapter 5:

Hoosier National

Jason and Zoe agreed to go hiking the following morning and then see David in the afternoon. One goal Jason had before leaving Bloomington was to climb the fire tower in Hoosier National Forest. It rose high above the virgin timber and provided a spectacular view across the rolling hills. And since it was a steep, difficult climb, you usually found yourself alone at the top with plenty of time to take it all in.

At around 7:30 am, Jason parked his van in front of Zoe's apartment. It was a room in an old house that had been subdivided into three apartments of which Zoe's was the smallest. While small, the location was great, on Second Street a few blocks from the busy central hub of Bloomington, Kirkland Avenue and its many restaurants, bars, and other college standards. It was also close to her job at Bloomington Bagel Company. Zoe had been waiting on the porch and ran down the front steps carrying a well-worn Tibetan crafted bag and her usual hiking ensemble of cut-off jean shorts, hiking boots, and a flowing white embroidered shirt. Hiking was one of her favorite things and most weekends she was off with friends traipsing through the woods. There was a group at the Bagel Company that always seemed to be venturing into the wild. She smiled at Jason as she reached the bottom of the steps and pulled open the passenger door to the van.

"Hello there, Zoe," Jason greeted her.

"Hi." Zoe looked him in the eyes with a bright face. She was excited. The van was already moving forward as Jason continued.

"Ready to climb the tower?" Jason was eager and ready. "I've wanted to do this forever and just never seemed to make the time."

"I'm ready, but it's not my first time," she admitted. "I went there a lot last year. But I haven't been in a while and I am excited; the view from the tower is amazing. I even brought us a thermos of coffee to drink at the top!" She held up a well-worn green Stanley thermos that had been her grandfather's.

"Fantastic," Jason replied and they drove on.

It took about 15 minutes to make their way out of Bloomington into the rolling countryside of southern Indiana, and finally their destination, Hoosier National Forest. Hoosier National Forest covers a wide swath of southern Indiana and contains over 260 miles of trails. It is a glimpse of the forest life that covered most of Indiana before it was swept aside by fields of corn and the progress of civilization, vast forests that had spread south from the Ohio River all the way north to Lake Michigan. In Hoosier National you could veer off a path and soon find yourself completely enveloped by nothing but forest. Sit still a few minutes and animal life would burst around you – birds, squirrels, foxes, deer, and all sorts of crawling, flying, digging creatures. It was a natural wonder that required nothing of you but the effort and desire to be amongst it.

Once Zoe and Jason had turned into the National Forest area, it was a three-mile drive on a double-lane county road and then a turn onto an unpaved fire road that meandered through the woods, until finally reaching the parking area where you could then get out and walk to the fire tower. There were a few other cars when they arrived at the parking area but the travelers seemed long gone, probably hiking deep into the woods via the trail head that was just a few yards from the tower. It looked like there was no one up on the tower platform. They were lucky; it should be theirs alone.

The Hickory Ridge Fire Tower was the last remaining fire tower in Hoosier National Forest. It was listed in the National Historic Lookout Register, and unlike many other similar structures, it was still open to the public. The tower consisted of 133 steel steps that rose 110 feet into the sky. Built in 1936, Hoosiers and other visitors had been climbing to the top for decades to experience the true bird's eye view. Today, Zoe and Jason would climb its sturdy structure and find a little fresh air and spectacular views, and maybe something more.

Zoe strapped the Tibetan bag over her back, and Jason retied his shoes. They looked at each other when they were ready to climb and smiled. Smiles were something they both had been experiencing much more of since yesterday. Now, they were ready to go and find some more joy. More than anything it was a blessing to feel alive, like they were moving forward. Never underestimate forward momentum, a friend had once told Zoe and she was right. Zoe had been stuck in the dark for so long, it was only at a moment like this that she really understood the power of 'forward momentum.' Here in Hoosier National the dark seemed far away, it was time to go.

"Let's go, race you to the top!" Jason sprinted ahead and Zoe followed. The race lasted about 30 steps when the burning of lactic acid spoke loudly, "Slow down if you want to make it to the top." So they did and together began a slower, more deliberate pace.

While slower, their hearts still raced and there was little talking on the way up. Speaking isn't necessary though to draw one closer to another and as they climbed, never straying more than a few steps apart, each could feel the chance meeting of yesterday being bonded with the physical exertion of climbing. It was pure, a rhythm that is hard to find in the cacophony of the city. It was not young lust or a night on the town glad-handing. No, it was just two people climbing together for a goal and an adventure to share. With about 15 steps to go the destination was in site. They sped up which exponentially increased the burn of their legs and the fire in their lungs, but they bore on. They were almost at the top and the site of a journey's destination can overcome the simple pain of effort. By the time they reached the viewing bridge, they were starving for air and on fire with lactic acid. They collapsed on the platform, back to back, breathing hard, with big satisfied smiles. After a long minute of huffs, Jason spoke.

"We did it!" He turned toward her and then gave the Marine Corps cry, "Ooh Rah."

"Yes we did!" Zoe exclaimed, and as they slapped hands she gave her own high-pitched, "Ooh Rah." Zoe was alive, bright, all blue eyes and wild blond hair. Her worn hiking boots and white and weathered embroidered shirt completed the picture of a young lady completely in her element. It was in this moment that Jason fell in love with her, in all of her sweaty, exhausted, euphoric glory. But he couldn't do that, he immediately told himself; he had a trip to take.

They settled back and a few more silent minutes went by as they continued to catch their breaths. Breathing normally, they rose from the platform's deck to look across the expanse of forest. It was wondrous. They could see birds flying in and out of the treetops, and there was the sound, or the lack of sound. No cars, no people, nothing artificial. The hum of modern life was gone and you could hear nature breathing. Zoe opened the thermos to pour the coffee and they drew closer as she gave Jason his cup.

"Here you go, some Kona from work. It's not really worth what they charge, but it's sure good," she commented as she poured.

"Kona?" Jason asked.

"Kona, in Hawaii. They say it's the smoothest coffee you can get. It's the best we have." She took a sip and smiled.

"Sure smells great," Jason agreed. "Thanks for bringing it."

"Couldn't go on a hike without packing the java, plus the extra weight makes it a better workout." She looked around for a minute then asked, "What do you think of the view?"

"It's, I don't know, majestic," Jason searched for the right word. "It's like another world. I wish I had come here before. We have plenty of hills around Bloomington, but it still seems so, well, grounded. Up here it is like we are only a jump from heaven."

"Well, if you jump, I hope you can fly or else your next destination will be either heaven or hell!" Zoe winked an eye.

"I'll stay right here, thank you." Jason took a sip of coffee. "So weird that yesterday morning we didn't even know each other existed, and now a day later, we've met David and are up here in heaven." Jason turned away from

Zoe to watch a squirrel scampering through a tree. He was also trying hard to avoid the realization that he knew he had fallen in love with her once they reached the top.

What did that even mean? He thought. *I don't deserve love. I'm a monster. If she ever knew the truth about me, she wouldn't love me, she'd despise me. No, I can't love her.* So he kept burying the feeling, or at least tried. Like he'd buried everything else, the good and the bad.

Zoe hesitated a minute before she replied. Actually, she had known Jason existed before yesterday. They were both good at hiding things, especially Zoe. She knew very well who he was. It would have to come out later though. Too much pain in that reality, and today, today was wonderful. So why spoil it. So they continued, each holding a secret.

"Up here in heaven? This is better than heaven. It's real," Zoe explained.

"Not a heaven believer, huh?" Jason asked, not so sure himself.

"I would like to believe," she paused, "in something. But life has taught me there are no angels who are going to come save me and God doesn't seem to have much of a place for me in this world," she stated, eager to see how Jason would reply.

"I'd like to believe too," Jason said softly. "I used to believe, until Iraq. I prayed to God. Most of my friends prayed. Of course, most of those we were fighting were people who prayed, too, probably more than I did for sure. Monsters, but monsters who prayed." He paused and familiar faces rushed into his head. "Both sides suffered and the worst were the children in the middle of it all." Jason stopped for second and composed himself. He could see the bodies of children blown apart, others turned to dust and pink mist. "If there is a God, the only side he was on over in Iraq was death. After a while I just quit praying. Hate and vengeance seemed a better way to make it through a war."

"I used to pray," Zoe admitted, "but it seemed like the more I prayed, the worse my life got." It was true, she had walked through hell, and every time she asked God for help, it seemed like she was kicked in the face. "And it wasn't like I was a bad person. I didn't use drugs, I wasn't an easy girl, but life was just so hard. God didn't help me and I just can't believe in heaven. Seems like someone just made all that up to get people to believe in a fairytale." She took a drink of coffee and observed, "I guess it's a good scam for all the people making money off of those who need to believe in something supernatural."

"No kidding," Jason said with a smirk. "Did you see that new church they are building on the south side of town? A friend of mine calls it Six Flags over Bloomington!" It was indeed a very large church. Started in an old strip mall, it was moving to greener pastures and a new campus on the south side of town.

"A girl I know goes there. She's always talking about how 'relevant' it is. Relevant? What she describes are services more like *American Idol*. Bet they don't have priority seating for the poor," Zoe added sarcastically.

"Hypocrites, all of them," Jason agreed.

"Yes, they are," Zoe followed. Of course, it is always easier to point the finger at someone else in order to avoid looking in your own mirror. That is what pain does; it destroys the mirror and everything in this world just starts to seem as sick and tired as we are. There were gracious people at that church and much good was done because of its size and influence, but all Zoe and Jason could see is what they wanted to believe.

As the negativity quickly wore out, the conversation stalled. They had not come here to be negative and the line of conversation was beginning to uncover deep wounds. It was time to be quiet again.

Zoe topped off their cups and they finished the Kona while they leaned over the tower's railing. A bird with deep, brilliant red feathers and even deeper streaks of black settled next to them. Neither Jason nor Zoe moved for fear of scaring the bird. All three seemed to stare at each other, then as suddenly as it had come, the bird left.

"Wow," Zoe exclaimed to Jason.

"Wow is right. Did you see how deep those colors were? I didn't know red and black like that existed." He pondered for a moment, then stated, "That is real." Zoe nodded her head in agreement. Reaching the bottom of his cup, Jason looked at his watch and realized they had better get going if they were going to make it back to David's by noon like they had planned. Before they left, Jason added a thought:

"You know, David believes in all that God stuff. What do you think about that?" It was a question Jason had been stewing over since yesterday. As much as he liked David, it seemed their talks with him would inevitably turn to God and that had been a hard turn for Jason to make.

"I don't know about God, but after yesterday, I believe in David," Zoe revealed.

"Me, too," Jason agreed, just as eager to see David again as Zoe.

They made their way down the stairs of the tower, much more quickly than the trip up, and were soon back at Jason's van. They thought about going back to Bloomington for a shower before visiting David, but that would have meant a lot of back-tracking; so after stopping for a soda, they headed for their afternoon rendezvous at Sycamore Hill.

Chapter 6:

Griddlecakes

Jason and Zoe arrived at Sycamore Hill to find David on the west side of his house, at the edge of the clearing next to the forest, building what looked like a large shed. Seeing them approach, he stood up from where he had been hammering and wiped the sweat off his brow. He then grabbed a large glass of ice water, took a swig, and said hello.

"Hello there. Glad you all made it back." And he meant it. He was worried Zoe might not return.

"It's good to be here," Jason replied.

Zoe grinned with a nod of her head and they approached David who had taken a seat in the grass. He poured them some ice water and welcomed them to sit down.

"Have a seat, I needed a break." David had been up at 6 am working. "I've been working on this place all morning."

"What's it going to be, a shed?" Jason asked.

"Guesthouse," David answered, "a very simple guesthouse; I don't want people getting too comfortable!" David smiled and continued, "I receive a lot of visitors from out of town and I've been meaning to build this for some time. Years really, but I've always been hesitant to give the impression people were welcome to stay for very long. But it's gotten so busy, I really need to allow for some longer visits. Especially from as far as some people come."

He stopped to take a long drink of ice water. "Usually they just sleep on the grass in a sleeping bag or on my porch. It is time for something a little more comfortable than earth or wooden planks." He took a second to survey the construction and continued, "It will have some bunks, a wood burning stove, and a simple sink with a water pump." He paused for a second and ended with, "I guess I'm getting soft in my old age."

"Soft? I don't know about that. Are you really that busy with visitors?" Jason wondered.

"Well, what I call busy, 5 to 10 people every week or so when the weather is good and even a few when it's bad," David explained. "There was a group of three girls here this morning. We spent a few hours talking."

"Thanks for fitting us in," Jason replied, lightly sarcastic.

"No problem, my young pilgrims." David winked back, and then looked over at Zoe. "How are you doing, young lady?"

"I'm good thanks. The climb this morning was invigorating," she explained.

"The tower climb always energizes me too." David had been up the tower more than a few times.

"Amazing view," Jason concurred. "Zoe brought some coffee and we got a little Zen at the top."

"Great place for that," David agreed. Then he

reminded Jason and Zoe what was waiting for them inside the cabin, not that they had forgotten. "Well, then, you two should be ready for my griddlecakes. I know I am."

"You bet." Jason was ready to eat.

"I'll second that," Zoe announced, her little frame hollow with hunger.

"Well, then, let's go inside," David invited them. "The batter is made. I just have to pour it on the griddle and we will have hot cakes in no time." David rose and Jason and Zoe followed. In a few minutes the cabin was filled with the smoky aroma of hot griddlecakes and their plates were piled high with the mouth-watering treat covered in real maple syrup and butter churned from David's goat's milk. The first bite was a mouth-watering explosion.

"Oh my goodness," Jason exclaimed, saying each word slowly. "It's melting in my mouth. Literally, melting. The butter is so smooth and creamy. And the syrup is perfect, not too sweet."

"That's the goat milk butter," David explained. "And the maple syrup is as close to nature as you will find, straight from the tree. My trees." He was proud of his trees.

"They are amazing," Zoe agreed, before filling her mouth again. "The Spoon has got nothing on this." The Runciple Spoon had quality breakfast food, but fresh goat's milk butter and real maple syrup were not on any menu in

Bloomington except here at Sycamore Hill.

They all quickly cleared their plates and then David served up the coffee he had been percolating on the stove. Jason was completely satiated after the griddlecakes, and was now ready to continue yesterday's conversation.

"I really appreciate you taking the time to hear me out, David," Jason said humbly.

"You have been through a lot." David looked Jason in the eyes. "I'm glad you are here."

"I thought about what you said yesterday." Jason put his hands together. "You're right, I guess I'm not alone, I'm not the only one to have those questions, especially guys like me who've been in war. But where do I go from here?" Jason paused then continued, "I do feel better here with both of you, but what about later? What about months from now? What about when I am alone?"

"What makes you think you'll be alone? Chances are Zoe and I will still be breathing then." David smiled and so did Zoe.

"Yeah, I know, but we probably won't be together." Jason lowered his head and had a hard time looking at either David or Zoe.

"So what?" David answered right back. "I live out here by myself; it can get lonely sometimes, but even in the middle of winter when I have not seen a visitor in weeks, I always find a way to remember that I'm surrounded by creation and this helps remind me that I'm never really alone. Life is much bigger than what is right in front of us. We only forget that when we quit living. Life can get small and lonely quickly if we let it. I know. Even now, sometimes old despair will take over and I have to remind myself to keep moving forward."

"Well, I feel alone most of the time, so I guess I must have quit," Jason answered, a bit agitated at David's frankness.

"Maybe, or maybe you just realize that you can't muddle any longer." David hit the nail on the head.

"Muddle?" He wasn't sure what David meant by it, but it still rang true.

"Yes, most people muddle through life," David reflected. "It's easy to do surrounded by all the noise in the world, all the distractions that consume people. I don't think you realize what a gift you have received to be broken and forced to do something radical like customize a van or come see me. Most people are too paralyzed by the fear of leaving the normal to step out of the stream. Of course, out of the stream is where you usually find life."

"Never saw it that way." Jason shrugged.

"But that is exactly what you did," David continued. "You decided to live, even though you felt like you were dead. Most people don't do that; they just muddle. They know they are not living, they know they are lonely, yet they allow the world to push them along. They spend enormous amounts of psychological and spiritual energy trying to avoid pain and being safe, which of course is a battle you can't win." He stopped for a drink. "When the pain does come, and it will for everyone, the world has a host of shiny things to mask the truth – from drugs to sex to television to technology and a million other seemingly innocent distractions and noise."

"Yeah, I noticed you embraced pioneer living. So I have to destroy the cell phone to live?" Jason asked.

"Of course not!" David laughed, "But the odds that you don't have noise to get rid of is ZERO, and part of that might be how you use the phone, or the Internet, or whatever." David was no Luddite, but he understood how technology had made the lives of many so vapid and full of life-killing distractions.

"Easier said than done," Jason stated what he thought was obvious.

"It's not that hard," David assured Jason and then looked over at Zoe who before this had been sitting transfixed, but was now a bit puzzled. *First we talk about God, now it's technology?* Zoe thought, trying to make sense of it.

"Well, let me say this," David continued, "It's not that hard if you can focus on living and being human. Don't let anyone fool you. When you get sucked into television, video games, smartphones, whatever, you have allowed yourself to become less than human."

"How is that?" Jason asked. "And who gets to define what is human?"

"We do, of course. But you would not be here if you thought you were living," David pointed out the obvious, "and all we know for sure is what stares at us in the mirror. You know what is inside yourself. And look around you; do people really look happy? What is behind the smartphone or computer glare in their eyes? What do you think they see when they look in the mirror? If they can even bear to look in the mirror. The mirror reveals reality and reality can be a horror for some. As a result, people who aren't living do everything they can to avoid it." David looked over at Zoe then back at Jason. "More people need to face the mirror and be honest about what they see."

"Well, I don't even know where to start. If I looked in the mirror, I already know that I wouldn't like what I saw," Jason stated honestly, thinking of the hate and fear that dwelt deep within himself.

"Make something. Create." David picked up a scrap of paper that he had written some building notes on and turned it into an origami bird as he spoke. "Start simply. The most basic meaning of life is to create. It can be as simple as this little bird here. It was a scrap, now it is something meaningful." He put the bird down as Zoe and

Jason leaned closer to listen and look at the bird. "More than anything, that is what has kept me here all these years. The constant creation and cycle of life, from building a new shed, to taking care of the path from the road, to the animals and trees and flowers. Surrounded by life and cut off from the noise that consumes people, it's hard to feel alone and when you do, it passes. When you live honestly, it is much easier to take account of yourself and your life. You can be fully human."

"So, do I have to move into the woods to be happy?" Jason wanted to know, "Or to be fully human? Whatever that means."

"Of course not," David gently clarified. "We all have different destinations, for some it's the woods, for others, far from the woods. The action everyone needs to take is a journey toward honesty, introspection, and simplicity. You must give yourself time away from the noise so you can find out what you are supposed to be creating. It could be art, literature, carpentry, a family, a journey, or a combination of them all. Once you figure that out, you focus and get rid of as many distractions as you can. And the object of our creativity can change, do not be afraid of the change. The goal is not a thing; it is an action, a way of life, the object of which in many ways isn't important. This origami bird might be as valuable as the new tree I plant. Your wilderness might be in the middle of the woods or the middle of a city or right where you already are. Life's passion has few boundaries once you find it."

Zoe joined in. She wanted to believe, but her darkness was never more than a thought away.

"To be honest, I feel too, I don't know, dirty to create anything." She didn't just say it; it seemed to have come from a very deep place and was spoken as if the words had escaped a tortured pit. She had once taken up painting but all that she could put on the canvas was pain. It was the ugliness inside her and she couldn't bear to see it so she had stopped. Yet, David had reminded her she still felt the urge to create. If only she didn't feel so dirty, so unworthy.

"Dirty?" Jason questioned, suddenly very concerned about his friend Zoe.

Zoe didn't answer and just kept looking at David.

"Zoe, some of the best things ever created came from the dirt," David said gently. "Just read the Bible. It's not about perfect people; it's about sinners who became saints and the man they crucified at the center of it all. Adam and Eve, Abraham, King David, the Apostles, Paul, you name it; grace came to dirty people." He moved closer to Zoe and put a hand on one of her knees. "God can forgive anything. The dirt only keeps us from creating when the guilt of the dirt makes us stop living. Hell is complete isolation, feeling separated from everything, especially God.

Hell is the opposite of creation, it is destruction." David was trying to help her see that she was closer to God than she realized. The pain could actually be a bridge to life.

David leaned back and gave Zoe and Jason a chance to chime in, but they were silent and their faces made it clear they wanted him to continue.

"You are not dirty, Zoe." David tried to reassure her. "You are human. Don't let the airs people put on fool you; everyone has dark secrets they are ashamed to reveal. Everyone that is except the truly evil. Give yourself over to evil and you will feel no regret, no shame, and no conscience. But you will be a devil. Allow yourself to be forgiven and to forgive, and while you will feel an even greater need to keep confessing all the faults that plague us, you will find peace." He let that sink in for a moment then continued, "Like the thief on the cross who asked Jesus to remember him, 'Jesus, remember me when you come into your kingdom,' be honest about who you are and instantly a door to heaven opens."

"Heaven." The word jolted Zoe. "What's heaven?" The darkness was battling Zoe and the light struggled to reign.

"Heaven is right in front of you." David wanted to help her see, help her find forgiveness and freedom. "Heaven is in God. Creation is ultimately the signature of God and when we allow ourselves to be part of that we can experience a glimpse of what it means to be divine. After all, Christ more than anything is a living symbol that God wants to be with us, and us with him. Even the good book says we were created in his image, God's image."

"And it's better than that," David revealed, "when we draw close to God we draw close to all the others who have learned to love and be with God. We are not alone. We could be suffering in a prison, struggling to raise kids, grieving over a lost friend, dealing with trauma, tragedy, you name it, in the pain we are not alone and will never be alone and that is where we find hope."

"Do I have to believe in God?" Zoe asked and Jason nodded his head with her. Neither had come to see David to answer that question affirmatively. They had wanted answers, but not what they saw as preachy answers. "God" still seemed so preachy to her.

"At this moment?" David smiled. "No. But you will. You can't look in the mirror, begin to create, and search your soul with humility without coming face-to-face with God. It's not about whether we like God, or understand God, or believe in God. He just is, whatever we may think about him."

"I'm just not sure. I think I'd hate him before I'd believe in him," Zoe stated as the horrors of her life flashed in her head.

"Well, then don't fight for an answer," David

suggested warmly. "You know I am right about how you have been living and what you need to do. There is a light tugging on your soul. You would not have come back if there wasn't. Focus on that and the answers will come. Answers you can believe in." The words carried weight because it was obvious that David totally and completely believed. He walked the talk. But there was more than that. There was a light in David's eyes most people didn't have. It was a fire that warmed and seemed to come from a very deep, even heavenly, place – a glow more convincing than any argument or book.

"I think I want to believe David. I just can't. Not yet," Jason said honestly, and with even a bit of sadness. Feeling unsettled, he looked at his watch and then over at Zoe. "Guess we better be going?"

Zoe had been waiting for that request; she needed time to process David's words. "Yeah, we probably need to get back." She rose from where they had been sitting and Jason joined her. It was time to go.

"You two come back anytime. I would love to see you again before Jason takes off." David knew this conversation wasn't over and it needed to be resolved before Jason left on his trip.

"We'll be back." Jason looked over at Zoe as he spoke and she nodded. "Really, I want to believe, it's just so hard. I guess I didn't realize how much God was tied up in all of this."

"I know," David answered and put his arm on Jason's shoulder as they all began to walk toward the road and the van. "I really know Jason. I couldn't believe either. It took Sycamore Hill to help me believe again. If you can come back I'd be happy to share some more."

Zoe and Jason were halfway down the path to the van when Zoe stopped. She had one more question that needed answering today.

"Can you wait for me by the van? I need to ask David something," Zoe asked Jason with a very clear *I need to do this alone* look in her eyes. Jason didn't need an explanation.

"Sure, Zoe. I'll wait for you."

Zoe walked back to Sycamore Hill where David was kneeling down in his tomato patch. She approached and called out as David turned toward her.

"David, I have something else I wanted to ask you."

"Sure, Zoe." David rose and walked toward her where they met in the middle of Sycamore Hill's clearing.

"It's about God," she stated and her lips started to quiver. Tears burst upon her face as she finished the question, "How could God just watch and do nothing when I was being raped? Nothing. How could I ever believe in someone who would do nothing?"

Zoe began to shake and David hugged her. He did not speak right away and just held her. When the sobs stopped and she seemed settled, he pulled away from the hug and began to answer.

"I don't know, Zoe. I've asked myself that question a million times. So have many others who have come here like you. Especially when life has been a horror." David stopped for a second to think and continued, "I know how I answered that question. It took a lot of anguish and time spent on my knees, but I think God was right there with me when all my suffering was happening. Just like I believe he was there with you. He was suffering with you, probably as gutted as you that his creation had resulted in your tragedy.

"This world he created isn't magic, and the purpose is not for us to avoid pain. It is for us to be free and exercise that freedom to follow God. To always intervene to stop pain would create a world far from free; in fact, it would be a world of make believe, of flesh and blood robots, a world not worth creating in the first place. To make sense of it, we have to keep looking to God's son; he suffered and promised suffering for those who follow him, and for those who don't follow him. The reality of death requires suffering. Free will means we will suffer – from our decisions, from others' decisions, from the cycle of nature. Everyone gets hurt.

"I have seen miracles, Zoe, but it's not often I actually pray for one anymore. What I pray for every day is the humility to follow and to live with purpose, for others the grace to do the same, and for God to bring all of those here who would benefit. When you follow God with purpose and grace, it is better than a miracle or a life free of pain; it is truly living in the spirit of creation and the Creator. And anyway, miracles are God's choice, not mine. When I do find myself praying for a miracle, the impulse to pray for it always seems to come from someplace else, as if God planted a seed and I'm responding to it. You see, more than anything, a walk of faith is a response; we become followers and listeners, not askers."

David finished and they stood quietly for a moment. Zoe wasn't sure what to say. David helped her.

"You don't have to believe any of that right now." David gave her another big hug. "I hope we will have more of these talks, even after Jason leaves. We'll work it out together."

"Thanks, David, I'd like to believe God was there with me," Zoe said hopefully.

"He was. He was with you, and he is with you now." David turned in the direction of the van. "Now you have a ride to catch."

"Yes, I do. Thank you, David." Zoe smiled and turned to jog back to the van where Jason was waiting.

Chapter 7:

How Would You Live?

David was alone. It was only a few months after his family's death and he had been spiraling down an ever-darker hole. It was an abyss that had sucked all the goodness from his life – his family, his job, his faith.

He lived in a small town west of Chicago, Wheaton, where he had worked as a financial manager for almost a decade and was quickly becoming surrounded by the sprawling Chicago suburbs. David and his wife had picked Wheaton because it was close to work, seemed like a great place to raise a family, and was near a large popular church, Wheaton City Church, which was filled with upper middle-class citizens, most of whom lived on Wheaton's old, tree-lined streets in grand, stately homes. Wheaton Church, as the members called it, had a myriad of activities for children, was a good place to network for his burgeoning financial management business, and he and his wife quickly made friends. Much of life in Wheaton was centered on the local Christian college, Wheaton College, called by some the Harvard of Christian higher education. For almost a decade, David and his family had made it home; in many ways, it was a mid-eighties version of a 1950s Norman Rockwell painting.

After the accident and as everything fell apart, he attended Church more and more infrequently, and when he did, the spectacle of the large community just seemed hollow. Everyone was trying so hard to live the American dream that he had lost – big house, manicured lawn, two kids, nice car, long summer vacation – that it just made him more alone with his pain and despair. He could care less about the American dream. If he couldn't have his family back, he wanted none of it.

Thoughts of suicide and the desire to die became constant ideations. He wanted to be with his family, and the only way that could happen was through death. Making matters worse, he was on the verge of losing his job with all the days off he had taken. Unpaid bills piled up on the dining room table, and for the last few weeks, he had not even bothered to open the mail. *Why open the mail, or pay bills,* he thought. *I'll be dead soon anyway and this all will go away.*

As the days wore on and he finally lost his job, he rarely left home. His beard grew, he rarely showered, and he subsisted mainly on soda pop and potato chips. It was only when supplies ran low that he would leave home and encounter civilization. At the grocery store he would do all he could to avoid eye contact, even with the checkout girl. It was always a quick visit, toilet paper, chips, soda, and maybe a few other things he threw into his cart as he made his way through the store. He would usually head straight home after shopping, but occasionally old habits would kick in and he would stop for a cup of coffee or breakfast at what had once been a favorite café, Jonesy's. Once, because now he had no favorites of anything. Any joy had completely slipped from his grip.

He didn't feel like feeding himself, so he made his way to Jonesy's and found an empty seat at the end of the counter where the waitress greeted him with a warm smile. With his long hair, bushy beard, and hushed voice, she did not recognize what had once been a regular customer.

"What can I do for you?" she asked genuinely. Denise had worked at Jonesy's for over a decade and loved her job and the people she served. At home was a loving husband who worked on cars and two kids who were both in junior high school. She had a good life.

"Just some coffee and a cheese omelet with peppers," David requested.

"You got it." She scribbled down his order. "How about some water?" came the standard question.

"Sure," he answered, still looking down at the counter top.

Denise walked away, quickly returned with the coffee and water, and then moved on to a young couple who had just sat down. David poured creamer in his coffee and started to sip on the hot brew. He was staring a hole through the counter and didn't notice the stranger sit down next to him until he started speaking.

"How are you doing?" the man asked. He was non-descript – in his late forties with pepper hair, khakis, and a polo shirt. He was clean-shaven with dark-rimmed glasses.

David turned to look, paused, and then acknowledged the greeting. "I'm okay," he lied.

"That's just great. I love Jonesy's, been coming here for years." The man looked around the café as if every corner held a special memory.

David nodded politely. If the man had indeed been coming here for years he sure didn't recognize him. David's omelet arrived about the same time as the stranger's coffee. That was all he had ordered, coffee. David took a few bites, and then the man continued.

"Look a little rough, friend," the man stated the obvious just as a piece of omelet fell in David's beard as he ate, "been there before myself."

David just nodded in reply, not looking up as he sipped from his coffee.

"Yep, I had that look when I got back from Korea," the man continued, "seems like forever ago. I'd fought in the Chosin Reservoir and lost many of my friends, including a couple of my toes." The stranger grinned, took a long drink of coffee and then continued, "The worst was when they attacked in the middle of a below zero night. It was early in December of 1950. We ended up fighting face-to-face with bayonets and frozen hands. It was inhuman." He wasn't grinning any longer.

David looked up, and then coldly asked of the talkative stranger, "Why are you telling me this? Do I know you?" He wanted an answer, but not really. He planned on listening whatever the reply. He hadn't spoken to anyone in weeks and he didn't really mind the noise. *But man, what a strange conversation,* he thought.

"No, you don't know me. I just thought you might want to hear a story, friend." The stranger paused to see if that appeased David before beginning to tell his story, "One night I woke to a scream. Near me was my best friend, Bob Wilson. By the time I got close he was dead with a knife stuck in his throat. His eyes were wide open and his mouth was stuck in a scream. The Chinese had sent a suicide fighter to sneak in and kill a sleeping Marine in order to terrorize the rest of us. Let me tell you, it worked." He finished his cup of coffee then carried on, "I went almost a month after that never really sleeping. Not until we got pulled off the front line."

"That's horrible," David commented as he thought about his own horrors.

"The worse thing was that Bob had saved my life twice."

Looking in the man's eyes, David could tell he could remember his friend like it was yesterday and they had just left each other. The man explained further, "He had a really nice family and they were always writing and sending pictures. About all I did before the war was drink and fight. I didn't even have what I would call a family.

More like a hillbilly tribe of southern Indiana rock cutters."

David had stopped drinking his coffee and was now totally engrossed with his new friend. He had never experienced war, but the stranger was still pushing buttons.

"It didn't seem fair that Bob was the one who got it. I really began to hate God after that. Not that I had believed in him much before. I started thinking about every friend who had died, every person I had killed. Their faces swirled in my head non-stop. Soon, I just wanted to die. I began to do everything I could to get killed, and I killed as many of them as I could. Kill, kill, kill. I was consumed by death." He looked directly into David's eyes. "I thought I was a monster."

He paused a minute. David didn't say a word.

"Then when I got home it got worse. I couldn't sleep; I'd walk the streets looking for a fight. I'd have a dream and Bob himself would come and say, 'you should be dead.' I would have died if not for a book title I saw, as silly as that sounds." He took another drink. "I was looking around a bookstore and saw a title that said, *How Would They Have You Live?* I'm not even sure what the book was about or who wrote it. I just immediately thought about Bob and the words struck deep, *how would he have you live?* You are alive, you fought for each other, how would he have you live?"

David suddenly felt the air come of out of him. He

thought of his family. How would they want him to live? *Not like this,* he thought. The stranger answered his own question.

"Not how I was living, that was for sure. Pretty easy answer really. I suddenly felt selfish and dropped to my knees, right there in that bookstore. My legs collapsed. I vowed that whatever it took I would live. I asked God to help me. That is what I owed Bob, that is what I owed myself, to live.

"I left the store and the first thing I did was shave and shower. Then I quit the job I hated, put my house up for sale, and started planning what I would do next. I haven't looked back since."

David sat there, not saying a word. The oddness of the situation hit him again. *Who was this stranger? I just wanted breakfast.*

The stranger finished up his coffee, threw some cash and change on the counter, and got up to leave. David was stunned at this point.

"You take care of yourself, son," the man said warmly with a hand on David's shoulder. "We all will go through some hell. What we owe ourselves and those we love is to make the absolute most of this life. There is no shame in that; that is what they would want. That is what you would want if you'd been the one to die and leave them behind."

David just nodded. The stranger was right, one hundred percent right. Then the man left as suddenly as he had arrived. *Was this a dream?* The waitress interrupted his question.

"Can I get you some more coffee?" she asked.

"No thanks, you can bring the check. By the way, do you know the man I was just talking to? He said he was a regular."

"Regular, I've never seen him before." She looked out the doorway the stranger had just left.

"Are you sure? He said he has been a regular for years."

"Years? Darling, I've worked here for almost 10 years. I've never seen him before. Sorry." She walked away to get David's bill and David sat in complete wonder. *Who was that and what had just happened?*

The waitress returned and David paid his bill. He felt stuck to the seat. *Who was that guy?* After a few minutes of confusion he got up and left Jonesy's. While unsettled, he had resolve. He would start living again.

Walking home with his groceries under a beautiful blue sky, a plan began to develop. He had to get away from the city, there were too many reminders of life before the tragedy, and he had never really liked Wheaton anyway. It was convenient, but something about it always seemed less than real. He remembered as a child visiting land his grandfather owned in the middle of the woods near Bloomington, Indiana. Little more than an old cabin and an outhouse, he was pretty certain it had remained in the family, but rarely used by anyone anymore. *What was its name,* he tried to remember? *Oh, yeah, Sycamore Hill.*

He liked that name, Sycamore Hill. Seemed like a good place to learn to live again. His family would be happy he was in the woods; his kids had always loved camping and his wife had dreamed of moving into a rural home someday. David had plenty of money in the bank, from his savings as a financial manager and his wife's life insurance policy, so a job wasn't a concern at the moment. If Sycamore Hill was what he remembered, something told him it might just work out.

It didn't take long to find the cousin who owned the property and they quickly settled on a price of $45,000. That seemed fair and left David plenty of money to do some renovations and get settled. Thanks to the stranger, and the vision of Sycamore Hill, he was ready to try and live again.

Chapter 8:

Crazy Demons

Zoe was alive, but she wasn't living. The last couple of days with David and Jason had given her hope, but it had also opened doors. Doors to horrors she had spent a lifetime trying to lock away. The horror of a little girl abused over and over by a man everyone else in the family trusted. A little girl who never truly grew up and was always looking over her shoulder with fear. A young teenager living in Indianapolis who had been assaulted walking home from the grocery store where she had been sent on an errand by her mother. It was a brutal sexual assault that left her hospitalized. Unfortunately, the man was a first time offender, had a good lawyer, and after five years of good behavior in prison was released. The moment she realized he would soon be paroled, Zoe spent every moment of every day in panic, expecting him to spring upon her at any moment. That was, until he was gone, killed in a bar fight that she wished she could have seen, and participated in. It was the only justice she had ever felt, and while it made her happy for a moment, it was bitter. He was dead and she was still in hell.

All the horror and all the effort to keep the horror hidden had broken Zoe. One minute she was living and the next she couldn't leave her room because she was overcome with fear. She always seemed to be letting people down, never reaching the potential people told her she had. She had started cutting herself after the assault as a teenager and that had led to thoughts of suicide. She wanted the pain to end. Her soul got sicker and she began to completely disassociate from herself. She would wake up in the middle of the night lost after walking out of her house into neighbors' yards, in the street, and other places she shouldn't be. She could never remember how she had gotten there. It was a dream you woke up from some place other than your own bed. She thought it was her soul searching for death.

Arriving home after the day spent with Jason and David, they came. The climb up the tower and the conversation with David had given her hope. But hope usually brought with it the demons of disappointment, failure, and despair. Hope had been vanquished by darkness so many times in her life that hope itself had become nothing but an omen of pain. Hers had become a world where hope could not be allowed to exist. Afraid that today's hope would bring the demons again, she opened a bottle of wine and drank herself to sleep. Unfortunately, the wine was a red river of deceit the dark ones rode upon. She woke to their faces.

Ghosts filled her room, deathly creatures with flowing robes and pretty smiles. "Follow us. Come with us," they repeated, "you'll feel better. We'll help you feel better. Just cut yourself and let it all fade away." They made death sound so peaceful.

Zoe didn't want to resist. She wanted them to take her and she followed them out her front door. They continued to call and she followed. Sycamore Hill, Jason, and David had not yet replaced her desire to be free of the world. The pain was too much and the last couple of day's reprieve seemed to have only energized the darkness she had been trying to escape. "Follow us, sweet Zoe. Follow us," they called, and she did. Over a lawn, behind a house, toward a university town street that was busy even in the late hours of night.

Then, peeking from behind a large Victorian home, she saw them – the grandfather who had stolen her innocence; the man who had finished where her grandfather had left off. *But weren't they dead? Oh my God! They couldn't be killed. Only I can die. I have to die. I have to run.* Zoe ran. Toward the street, in the dark. The car that would hit her would never see her coming. In the dark, she was a ghost.

Zoe's tiny body ran faster and faster. She screamed louder and louder. The traffic ahead of her was a blur and the demons flying overhead called her home, "Keep going, Zoe, keep going." Zoe came. She was ready. She lunged into the traffic.

"Zoe, stop! What are you doing?!" It was Jason. He yelled as he lunged toward her. The cuts on Zoe's arms had not gone unnoticed. Climbing the tower and in the car, he had seen them whenever her shirtsleeves fell back. Together with glimpses of pain he had seen creeping across her face, it was clear that she was in a dark place. After dropping her off and processing the conversation with David, he couldn't stop thinking about Zoe and her anguish, and the fact that he was in love with her. He couldn't shake her.

He fell asleep soon after getting home then woke late in the night with a raging thought, *Zoe is in trouble.* He didn't know where the voice came from, but he didn't hesitate. He jumped out of bed and headed for Zoe's. Driving down Kirkland Avenue, about to turn onto Second Street, he saw her running toward the traffic. She was in a manic trance, screaming, yet her eyes looked calm. A deathly scream and a calm face, she was a ghost. He pulled over the van, jumped out, and ran, grabbing her just before she lunged into the street and in front of a delivery van.

"Zoe, Zoe. Listen to me. What are you doing?" he pleaded, folding her into his arms. She slowly came out of her dissociative state as he held her. She began to look around, then back to Jason; he could see the confusion and the pain in her eyes. Most of all, he could see the hopelessness and despair.

He continued to hold her, and whispered in her ear. "You are not alone, Zoe. You are not alone," Jason reminded her as she buried her head in his chest and began to cry. After a few moments, he led her back to the van where he helped her climb in, let her be still for a few minutes as she curled up in his passenger seat, and then took her home. She was sound asleep when they arrived at her house. He carried her inside, put her to bed, and then sat down in the chair across from her bed where he waited in the dark while she slept. It was a long and hard sleep. Jason stood watch the rest of the night, never once nodding off. He was in Marine mode, on a mission to protect.

What a couple of days, he thought to himself in the silence of Zoe's room. *One minute I'm on my way to leaving town, the next I'm here holding watch over my new friend. What is next?*

He felt at peace keeping watch over Zoe. He knew what David meant about creating something. It really just meant caring about something or someone outside yourself. Creation could be an act of kindness, a small word said to a vulnerable person at their most vulnerable time. It was love. Each moment in the room watching Zoe was meaningful. At that moment, his vigil over her was the most important thing in the world, and all he had had to do was get out of bed and go find her. Wasn't that most of life, just overcoming our fears and disappointments, our guilt and our shame, to show up, even when we didn't know who or what was calling us to show up?

Zoe woke up at about 8 am, much earlier than Jason had expected. As she stretched in bed and looked around her room, surprisingly, she was not startled to see Jason sitting in the corner. She had a vague memory of the evening and it made sense that he was there. He greeted her.

"Hey there. How are you feeling?" Jason asked and stood up to move closer.

"I'm okay." She yawned. "Still tired."

"I found you running toward Kirkland last night if you're wondering why I'm here. For some reason I didn't think you'd really remember." He filled her in, "I brought you home and put you to bed."

"Thank you. Thank you so much, Jason." She wanted to jump out of bed and hug him forever, but she couldn't let herself. "Sorry you had to see me like that. Sometimes I just black out and end up in the craziest places."

"I figured that wasn't your first time," Jason acknowledged.

"No, it wasn't." Zoe lowered her head.

"You hungry?" He was famished and figured they should get out of the house.

"Starving as usual," she answered quickly.

"Let's walk over to the Spoon, I'll buy," he offered. "I'll wait outside so you can get dressed." Zoe was touched at his thoughtfulness and dressed as quickly as she could. Her closet was spare, but interesting. She shopped at the local secondhand store, The Purple Cactus, and what she did have was full of colored personality. She grabbed a yellow sundress with purple and green embroidered flowers, slipped on her sandals, and walked outside to meet Jason. A hopeful thought stuck in her head, "You are not alone, Zoe. You are not alone."

They found a corner table at the Spoon where they could talk and both ordered a coffee and scrambled cheese eggs. The coffee soon arrived and as they waited for their eggs Jason thought he would start the morning with some lighter conversation after the gravity of the previous night.

"I tell you what, all this talking with David has got me stoked for my van trip out west." Wide vistas and virgin frontiers appeared in Jason's imagination. "There is no telling who or what I'm going to stumble across," he chuckled, "but good lord, I haven't even left Bloomington yet."

Zoe was excited for him, although she would miss her new friend. *Or was he more than a friend,* she thought. A voice inside wanted to go with him, yet, she knew it was a trip that she wasn't ready to make. She needed more time. And that felt okay. Somehow she knew this was only the beginning with David.

"It's going to be an adventure you'll never forget. I'm happy for you." Her eyes were proof she meant it. "I've thought about traveling."

"Where to?" Jason asked, hoping maybe she would say *in a van out west!*

"I've always wanted to go to France," she explained. "I signed up for an au pair service last year. I mulled over an offer from a family who want someone to teach their children English. They live in the wine country."

"Wine country. Cool. Are you going to try and go?" Jason asked.

"I almost committed a few months ago, then changed my mind. Now I'm not sure." What she didn't tell him was that, at first, she had not committed because she had decided to kill herself. She did reveal the second, most recent reason. "Now I'm starting to think I have some stuff to finish here. I don't want to feel like I'm running. Maybe I can sign up for a French class while I finish school if that is what I'm supposed to do. And then there is David. I think I have a lot more to learn from him before I leave."

Jason was thrilled to hear Zoe dreaming. As scary as last night had been, it was like she woke this morning outside of her shell. The waitress brought their eggs and they took a few bites, both famished after that long night.

"Man, those are good," Jason said with satisfaction.

"They sure are," Zoe agreed.

They took a few more hungry bites, and then Jason focused back on Zoe.

"Whatever you do, as David said, just keep moving forward," Jason encouraged her. "I'm beginning to think that it doesn't really matter what we do in life as long as it is meaningful."

"You might be right, look at David," Zoe began to observe. "If you told most people about him they would think he had nothing, a strange man living alone. Even crazy. But the truth is that he has everything, even when he has nothing," Zoe paused then said a little louder, "I want that."

"You warming up to God?" Jason smiled.

"Maybe. David has something and I want the same thing. The same peace. If that is God, so be it. I've made rasher decisions." She laughed.

"Me too," Jason added, then took a sip of coffee.

"Want to go back out there today?" Zoe suggested. "I have a little money saved up and thought we could get him something to help with his new shed." Zoe had good intentions but little building knowledge. "Any ideas?"

"This is going to sound silly, but how about some shingles?" Jason suggested, thinking this was an excellent idea. "I didn't see any stacked anywhere and they would sure help him keep that place dry."

"Great idea. David strikes me as the type who would appreciate a practical gift and shingles would be very practical for his new project," Zoe agreed and was excited to visit Sycamore Hill bearing gifts. David would appreciate it and it meant that a part of them would be there for a long time, or at least as long as the shingles lasted.

They finished up their eggs while talking about road trips and French wine. Upon leaving the Spoon, their next stop was Home Depot to get a couple bundles of shingles before heading back to Sycamore Hill. They were beginning to understand what it meant to live. Driving to David's from Home Depot, everything seemed more alive. The sky was bluer, the leaves were greener. They left the radio off and drove slowly through the woods toward Sycamore Hill with the windows down and listened. It was an easy thing to do, listen, because they were not alone.

Chapter 9:

We Three Kings

Arriving at Sycamore Hill, Jason and Zoe quickly realized that their gift of roof shingles would not be easily carried up the trail to David's. They couldn't help but look at David's old pickup truck and wonder if he would make an exception to his rule, "no vehicle beyond the entrance of the path."

It took both of them carrying one bundle at a time, and even then, it was an awkward struggle, almost as strenuous as climbing the fire tower. But they were doing it together and that was the most important thing, another opportunity to bond the friendship with physical exertion.

When they made it to the top of Sycamore Hill with the first bundle, David was nowhere in sight. They wanted to finish the job and quickly returned to the car without taking the time to see where he might be. When they made it back with the second bundle, they were happy to see David opening the first. When he looked up to see them coming there was a huge smile across his face.

"Thank you both, so much," he thanked them with obvious gratitude. "You didn't have to do this, shingles are not cheap."

"No problem," Jason answered. "We wanted to do something for you and figured this would help with the new guesthouse. It would be a shame to do so much work and have a leaky roof!"

"Yep, we figured you were the kind of man who would appreciate some good shingles," Zoe added with a grin.

"You are right about that, Zoe!" David did indeed like quality building supplies. "I have been working all morning, and I know how heavy those shingle bundles are to carry. What do you say we sit on the porch and have a drink? I'll go get some tea," David suggested.

"Sounds good," Jason answered.

"I'd love some," Zoe said with a dry throat.

David walked into the cabin while Jason and Zoe waited for him on the porch. The porch was raised about a foot off the ground and the front edge was a great place to sit. David returned and they sat down on the porch edge to enjoy the tea and each other's company. More importantly, Jason and Zoe had more questions for David. Jason was burning to leave on his trip but not before he'd digested a bit more of David's wisdom.

"Mind if I ask a few questions while we sit here?" Jason asked David. He knew David would oblige, but since they had just arrived, he wanted to be polite.

"Go ahead," David answered, "we have plenty of time."

"You know, David, I see what you mean by the whole 'creating' thing. Make something out of nothing and all of a sudden you realize that there is always an opportunity to do something good and worthwhile. But to be honest with you, in a lot of ways, I don't even feel like I deserve to live. What does it matter if I do something good?"

"Why don't you think you deserve to live?" David asked, although from the earlier talk with Jason and past encounters with other veterans, he had a pretty good idea why Jason felt the way he did. He had seen the familiar mask of guilt and shame the second he set eyes on Jason. It was a pain shared by many others, not just veterans, who had found their way to Sycamore Hill.

"It's what I did. All the horrible things that I did and was part of." Jason looked down. While the words were few, they said a lot. The business of war dealt evil on all sides. David gave him a moment, and then Jason finished. "I'm a monster. I can't tell you everything I did; you'd never look at me the same. Zoe too."

"You don't know that, Jason," Zoe spoke before David could. David then followed her up.

"It's like we talked about before, Jason. Knowing that you fought in that war, I have a pretty good idea why you think you are a monster; I don't need the details." And David didn't; he had heard volumes of war stories on Sycamore Hill. "The battle and the killing can be like a drug, hyper-adrenalin we crave even when it is destroying us and our friends." David paused for a second. "Killing another human being is unlike anything else and while it destroys our souls, it can give some a thrill like no other. It can bring the devil out of anyone, and when the devil comes and makes a home in our soul, we feel beyond redemption." David leaned a bit closer to Jason and put a hand on his knee. "Don't give yourself too much credit though; you don't have to fight in a war to feel beyond redemption. Whenever we sacrifice the goodness of another for our own self-will, we welcome hell into our soul. And there are plenty of ways people indulge self-will at the expense of another – fathers, mothers, brothers, sisters, friends, you name it – anyone has the potential to give in to the demons of selfishness and vanity."

"That, that's me," Jason stopped and started to cry. "I'm a devil, but I don't want to be anymore." Zoe held him and David gave him a moment to continue. Jason explained, "All those people I killed. The children. Every time I lie down and close my eyes they come. I just want them to go away," Jason pleaded. Zoe felt helpless to help her friend and looked up at David for an answer.

"Have you asked them to forgive you?" David asked.

"Forgive me. They are dead." *If it was possible, yes,* Jason thought, but they were dead.

"I found hope on my knees, Jason," David explained, thinking back all those years ago to the night he found peace and faith on Sycamore Hill. "That is the same place where you will find forgiveness. I know this is hard, but by unburdening your heart with us you are exposing those demons to light. Keep working through it, as hard as it has been and will be, until you can drop to your knees and find forgiveness. That is where the road to healing begins. On your knees you will find understanding. You will see that even though they have passed to the next life, you can still find forgiveness."

"But I'm a monster." Jason wanted to believe, but he didn't think monsters deserved forgiveness, or redemption.

"You are not a monster. You are human," David said firmly. "We all feel the pull of evil, and we all need redemption from something. Even monsters, and you are not a monster, were created by God in his image before they became disordered. Our choices can allow the evil one to take that image and turn it into a distorted figure that runs from God and desires for others to do the same. The dirtier you get, the harder it is to believe you can change. But thankfully, even the slightest hint of true goodness can turn us in another direction." David stopped and took a good long look around Sycamore Hill – the animals, the gardens, the quiet, the sky above – then he continued. "That is one of the main reasons people feel better when they come to Sycamore Hill. Surrounded by creation in its purest form, living off the land, one begins to feel part of it, regardless of how dirty their soul is. When you are out there amongst the noise of civilization, the world with all its dirt and all the other people living blind, we feel like we will never find anything worth living for. But here at Sycamore Hill we are able to see the reality the dirt hides. The reality that we were all created for a purpose and whatever that purpose is, and no matter how simple that purpose might seem to anybody besides ourselves, it has worth. Worth that can overcome the darkness and bring us hope."

"Worth, I sure don't feel like I'm worth much," Jason said without looking up at David. Zoe was still holding him and listening intently. She didn't feel like she was worth much either. Yet, together with Jason and David on Sycamore Hill, life had begun to mean something, to have value. She actually could understand what it meant to look forward to living.

"I have evil in me," Jason explained. "It won't leave. I promised myself when I came home from Iraq that I would never be a part of death again, but I couldn't escape. You know why I decided to go on this trip?" Jason asked David as he looked straight into David's eyes. He didn't look at Zoe because he was ashamed at what he had done, and the monster it had unleashed. "I'll tell you why. I killed again. I killed a man in a bar."

"You killed a man?" David asked and Zoe didn't move. "What happened, Jason?"

"I was in a bar up in Indianapolis where no one knew me. I just wanted to drink and be alone. A man sitting at the bar kept messing with this woman, and the harder she tried to ignore him, the more aggressive he became – grabbing her, coaxing her – you know how that goes. Well, no one said anything to him. I think he knew the bartender and was just allowed to get away with badgering women." Jason stopped and took a deep swallow, and then he continued, "Finally, I'd had enough and went over to tell him to stop. The next thing you know we are arguing, I'm yelling at him and the girl is yelling at him, and he is yelling at us both. All of sudden, he pushes down the girl, she hits her head on the bar and is knocked out; and then, before I can even reach over to pick her up, he lunges at me with a beer bottle. I didn't even have time to think. As he came at me, I swung up and hit him square in the throat. It crushed his larynx and as he fell he hit his head on the bar like the girl, only harder. By the time I checked for his pulse, he was dead."

"How did you avoid jail?" David asked, not hiding his concern nor his curiosity very well.

"An off-duty cop had seen it all and testified the man swung first, I didn't intend to cause undo harm, and that my actions were to protect the girl," Jason explained, mimicking the language used by the judge at his hearing. "He had been walking over from across the bar where he was playing pool to stop him, but I beat him to it. Thanks to his testimony, the judge dropped the case against me."

"Thank goodness for that officer," David observed. "As horrible as it is, you can't feel guilty for that. You protected that woman. That was not the act of a monster."

"Maybe not, but the monster came out. I didn't just protect her, don't you see? I liked it. In that moment, I liked killing him. I have caused too much death. When will it end?"

"Death will never end, Jason," David said bluntly but softly. "Never. I hate to be harsh, but in truth, your horror is no worse than anyone else's. We ALL are going to die one way or another, it is all tragic. It is all a horror. Physical death is the grim reality each one of us faces," he grabbed Jason's hand, "but that doesn't have to be the end."

"Really, death sounds pretty final to me," Jason smirked. "And it can't be much worse than the hell I'm living now."

"But that is where you are wrong," David gently corrected him. "You aren't living in hell, right now. In this moment, sitting here together with Zoe and myself, does it feel like hell?"

"No," Jason turned to look at Zoe and found himself smiling.

"Of course not." David shook his head. "Your hell has been living with all of this alone. When we are alone, not much seems real except for our pain. It doesn't just go away, but when we begin to fellowship with someone who cares about us it can sustain us until we find the answers we are looking for."

"But will it really make sense?" Jason asked, wanting to believe there was an answer.

"Probably not how you imagine. If you are like most people, what you are asking for is magic, a child's fantasy," David said as thoughtfully as possible; it was a hard thing for someone to hear. "We all want to search for a happy ending with no pain and where everything makes sense. That doesn't exist and it wouldn't be life if it did; it would be a comic book or a computer program. In fact, it would be its own kind of hell. It's what the devil is in the business of selling. You see, in hell, people do exactly what they desire. But desire leads away from God and desire is never satisfied, never quenched. It burns and when someone enters the eternal fire, in truth, it is exactly where they want to be. The punishment is God allowing them to be there, a place where corrupt souls can be cleansed by the only thing that cleans completely, fire. It is judgment in its purest form." David let it sink in for a minute then continued, "Evil comes to itself, especially the evil within us, unless we allow God to cleanse and sanctify us. Finding God means understanding that when we follow ourselves it leads away from God, but when we help others, when we listen for God instead of talking to God, we discover that the only burdens we really have are the ones we have placed upon ourselves. God's son showed us that he understands our pain, but his son also gave us hope and the way to overcome death, and with it, our pain. He gave us the path to life."

It was a lot for Jason to swallow, but after the events of the last few days it was becoming easier to believe. Zoe was soaking up every word. It had been a long time since she had trusted anyone, much less a man, and now here she was with two, and there was nowhere else she would rather be. David had done a lot of talking and Jason was the kind of guy who once he was ready to listen, kind of just wanted the facts. He wanted David to sum it all up for him.

"When all is said and done, what does it all mean?" Jason asked. "Why do you believe in God, and how did you get over your pain? I think I know, but the last couple days are really sort of a blur."

"What does it all mean?" Zoe asked, staring hard at David for an answer. "I can't make sense of my own life, much less God." She was as eager and desperate as Jason to figure it all out. The pain she was carrying would eventually kill her and she knew it.

"I came to Sycamore Hill broken, angry at everyone," David began. "I had studied every philosophical and theological argument for God and they all just led me to emptiness, cynicism, and anger. In spite of all the searching and reading, I couldn't intellectually believe in God by some proof. It all seemed like a fantasy. It took something profound, but ultimately, simple, to show me the way. It was here at Sycamore Hill, desperate and alone, that I found him," David paused and looked over at the spot where it happened. "I fell on my knees one dark night and prayed and realized I was not alone. As I walked forward in faith after rising from my knees, miraculous things began to happen. At least miraculous to me considering the hell I had been living." David stood up and waved his hand across the landscape of Sycamore Hill. "They were small things, but amazing gifts of grace. People found their way to me and I somehow knew exactly what to say to them. I began to feel closer to my family than when they were alive. Sycamore Hill became a paradise and the animals were friends, not just creatures. People like you came and in some weird, unexplainable way, it wasn't an accident. There was purpose and meaning to it all. It helped me see that God doesn't force us to do anything, but when we walk with him we meet others doing the same. We find opportunities to love and help each other, and this more than anything makes us feel like we are truly part of heaven. It is a journey where we experience God right now, a real experience, not just words in a book. Not theology, not an argument, but something real no person, no evil, can take away from us. You see, our lives are more than just dust and bones; we are already a part of heaven if we will just open our eyes and follow."

"Dust and bones, or worm food," Jason couldn't totally over-rule the cynic residing in him.

"Worm food?" David smiled at the synchronicity. He remembered feeling the same way. "Whatever you believe, I know this for a fact, life is better when we create and serve others. It is better when we decide to live. Life finds peace and joy when we focus on living and discover that finding true purpose is simple if we'll just listen. And if you do that, I truly believe you'll find God. He understands us better than we do ourselves."

"Don't you see how hard that is to accept?" Zoe sincerely asked, deciding to question David and interrupt his argument. "It's hard to believe that God can understand anything when as far as I know he is just some make believe concept. I've never heard him speak. He's never saved me from anything. Just the opposite; if there is a God he sat back and watched me be brutalized." It was still a hard thing for Zoe to say, even after revealing her anguish to David on the earlier visit. David tried to answer again.

"God's way is not easy, for him or us," David explained. "Nowhere in the Bible does it say that. It leads to peace and joy, but it's not easy. The requirement of communion with God is the possibility of excommunication from God. That means a world where evil and death serve as the alternative to life. It hurts us, I believe it hurts God. It's like I said about Jesus on the cross and his despairing cry. Not only does he understand, but he came to show us the way to God. It is the way of humility, of prayer, of love. There is no other way. In my life, the joy of God is when we walk with him to overcome and make peace with death. When you find this path you realize that death is neither the end nor the beginning of life, it is merely the transition from this world to the next."

"I wish I could believe all of that," Jason stated, "you sound so convinced."

"It's not about believing like me," David tried to explain. "It's about living, creating, giving to others, praying on our knees, and listening to the God who sent a son to suffer just like us so we'd know we were not alone in this cold universe. And then he rose to show us there was life after the suffering and death. He conquered death by death so that we may have life. Keep moving in the direction you are now and you'll understand. The walk of faith forgives us, redeems us, and reveals our true purpose. Keep moving, keep loving. That is the only thing that will convince you."

"I will. I'll keep moving and trying." Jason meant it. It was a lot to take in and reflect upon. He decided to save any more God questions for later, and after a long moment of no one talking, he took the opportunity to change the conversation a bit, "What do you think about my trip?"

"I think it's a great idea," David encouraged him. "A trip like that, done because you are looking for something, is always a great idea. Even if what you find could have been found right where you are." He stood up from the porch and continued, "Sometimes, we need a change of scenery to appreciate what we already have."

"That's why I've decided to stay here," Zoe joined in. "My plans of going to France or somewhere really just felt like running away. I guess if staying here was going to lead to bad things, running away might not have been such a bad option, but I feel like I have some things to finish here in Bloomington. Some good things," Zoe stated, and then paused before looking hopefully at David, "and maybe a few more visits to Sycamore Hill."

"That would be great, Zoe." David was relieved she seemed to have made it through the worst of his fears for her. "I would love for you to keep coming."

"I don't think I was really ready to leave on my trip before we found you," Jason revealed. "But now I'm ready.

I'm looking for something instead of running away. But I will be back."

"I will sure look forward to hearing about your adventures." David stood up and smiled. He knew they needed to chew some more on what had been said, and he had much more work to do that day. "Now, make sure to come back to say goodbye before Jason leaves town. I have some work to do and if I procrastinate any longer, I'll lose all motivation."

"I'll come back by before I leave," Jason assured him. "Thank you for everything. I have a lot to think about. The trip will be good for processing it all."

"No problem, it was my pleasure. You come anytime, now or 20 years in the future. Who knows where your trip will lead!" With that David stepped forward to give Jason and then Zoe a hug, "I will see you all later."

"See ya' later," Jason answered as he stepped off the porch.

"Bye, David," Zoe added and followed Jason.

As they walked down the trail back to Jason's van, they didn't talk. Both of their brains were working overtime. Intellectually, they didn't believe it yet, but their hearts were filled with hope, and love was beginning to show them that there was a purpose to the seemingly random madness of life. Jason had to make final preparations for his trip and Zoe was eager to begin making the most of her time in Bloomington however long that would be, but more than anything, they were eager to continue the journey to their own Sycamore Hill.

Chapter 10:

Flower

Sycamore Hill was work. David spent the first year mostly cleaning and planting, then the next couple of years building – pathways, bird feeders, updates to the cabin, hammocks, and chairs. It became a virtual Eden hidden just a few miles from Bloomington. He also worked on himself. The physical labor was good for the soul when the pain emerged, and the solitude was just what he needed to focus when down on his knees praying, or reading his Bible. He had also begun venturing out into town more often. He wasn't eager to rejoin the world, but he wasn't trying to be a hermit either. He got to know the workers at the local coffee shops he frequented and the staff at the supply store where he did most of his shopping. His old Ford pickup rambling up soon became a welcome site to his new acquaintances and even the ladies at the bank where he kept his money. Due to Spartan living, he was able to live almost completely off the interest of his savings those first few years. Living off the land for most things, his expenses were minimal. Also, the past growing season he had harvested enough food from his garden that he was able to sell a good bit at the local farmers market. Over the upcoming years, his reputation for some of the best local produce would grow and it would become one of his main sources of income as Sycamore Hill expanded and with it his increased need for income.

During his third year at Sycamore Hill, he ventured one day into town to get some flour from Blooming Foods. Since his favorite treat was griddlecakes, the organic wheat flour from there was the perfect base ingredient. Walking down the aisles of his beloved supply store, he noticed a young girl standing near his destination in Aisle 6. She was ragged looking to say the least, her clothes worn, her hair dirty, no makeup, bad skin, terribly skinny, but not the college hippie who tried to look that way on purpose. No, she looked like life had dealt her that hand and probably much more that couldn't be determined by her appearance.

"Excuse me," David interrupted her stare, "I need to grab some flour." She had been standing directly in front of the five-pound bag he had his eye upon.

The girl didn't say a word, she just sort of shifted her weight. David looked closer and her countenance smacked David in the face, she was a ghost. He ordinarily would have just turned and left, but this time he couldn't. He had to say something.

"Are you okay?" he asked.

She turned to look at him, but didn't speak. She was empty.

"Can I help you get something? What are you looking for?" He wanted to help.

"Just some food," she spoke slowly and simply.

"What exactly are you looking for? Can I help you find it?" The more David talked the more he wanted to help her.

"Anything. I don't have much money." She held out her hand and there was nothing but a few crumpled dollars. He leaned closer and noticed just how vacant and hollow her eyes were.

"Don't worry, I'll pay for it. Just put what you want in my cart." David had his flour so he followed the girl as she slowly shuffled down the aisles. She didn't grab much, and continued not to speak. Her choices were a strange mix, almost like she wasn't sure what to get – some onions, a loaf of bread, peanut butter, and a bag of apples. After they checked out, David asked if he could give her a ride somewhere. She didn't answer.

"Really, I don't mind, where do you need to go?" David wasn't about to let her walk anywhere.

"I don't need to go anywhere," she answered.

It was then that all the pieces came together and David realized that this young girl was probably homeless, traumatized in so many ways that only God himself knew all the pieces of her shattered soul.

"Why don't you come with me and have some griddlecakes?" David kindly suggested. "I don't live far from here. You can eat something and rest, or whatever you need."

She nodded her head and followed him out of the store and into his pickup. No doubt she had gotten into strange vehicles before. It was probably how she had arrived in town, and probably how she would leave. She was broken and just reacted to things, almost like an animal.

They drove back to Sycamore Hill and David left her alone with her silence. This poor girl had been living on the streets and he wasn't sure what to do with her. He had been at Sycamore Hill alone and conversations when he visited town never really got very deep. He wanted to help her, but he wasn't sure how or what to say. All he really knew now was that he wanted to feed her and provide her some comfort.

They soon arrived at Sycamore Hill. David parked the truck at the foot of the trail and they began the walk up to the cabin and gardens. He had decided early on that he wanted the cabin area to always feel isolated so he built a parking area by the road and would never drive or park the truck near the house unless he absolutely had to. He was glad he did, because once one reached Sycamore Hill, it was like stepping into a world devoid of modern technology, yet full of possibilities and wonder. As they reached the top of the hill together and the expanse of the clearing came into site, David saw the first sign of life in the girl's face. She looked around, and even though it wasn't very wide and her teeth didn't show, she smiled. The beauty surrounding them lit up her face. The feeders were full of birds; the flower garden was in bloom.

"Here, let's walk up to the cabin. I'll draw some water and you can get cleaned up while I make some griddlecakes. When we are done, there is plenty you can explore or you can just sit and relax at the cabin." The girl nodded her head and David went into the cabin as she sat down in the grass next to a bird feeder. One of David's old friends, a bright red cardinal, landed on her shoulder and then flew away after a few moments of perching. She watched it land in a nearby tree and her smile became huge, her face beaming with joy. David soon came back with a towel and a large bowl of water.

"Here you go. By the way, my name is David." David was surprised it hadn't come up, but maybe not so surprising considering how surreal the experience was. He didn't ask her name, but she answered anyway. After looking around as if she was searching for a reply, with a peaceful look across her face, she simply said, "I'm Flower."

David smiled at the introduction, "Well, hello there, Flower. Welcome to Sycamore Hill. The griddlecakes will be ready in a minute." Pleased to have made a new friend, he headed back into the cabin to finish the meal.

The rest of the day was a treasure to David. Flower ate her griddlecakes quickly and when she was done got up and hugged him. She then went outside and sat by the bird feeder, using the loaf of bread she had bought earlier to draw the birds closer. She fed them with crumbs and they flew around her, completely unafraid. She smiled. And smiled more. Birds of all types and colors swarmed and fed and used her like a perch. When the bread was gone they calmed down and stayed near her. A true Flower surrounded by birds.

David walked from behind his cabin where he had built a small greenhouse, holding a large red tulip he had taken from it. He walked up to Flower and asked her to help him with it.

"Flower, can you help me plant this tulip?" he asked, eager to make a bit of Sycamore Hill hers.

"I'll help you," she answered, one of the longest sentences she would say all day.

"I'll go get some potting soil I have mixed up in the back." David used compost and topsoil to create his own. "Why don't you pick a nice place for it and then dig a hole," David explained. "I'll be right back."

"Okay." She didn't have to move far. Just a few feet from the bird feeder next to some yellow tulips she dug a home for the red tulip. She placed it in the hole and when David returned she helped him pile in the potting soil.

Together, they patted down the dirt after which David poured some water from a steel watering pitcher.

"That looks great, Flower. You picked a good spot." He looked at Flower and clapped his hands together.

Flower smiled.

As the day wore on it was pretty clear that Flower had nowhere to go. When night came, David told Flower she could stay if she wanted and then brought out a sleeping bag and pad and put them on the front porch. Flower was happy to take him up on his offer and she naturally curled up on the porch in the sleeping bag. David said goodnight and just like that the day had ended. For the next few days, Flower stayed and helped David with chores and the garden. They didn't talk much, and David learned little about her. Only that she was from a small town in northern Michigan and she was making her way south to Florida. She liked Neil Young and the Grateful Dead, and when she could find a way, went to their concerts. Most of the time she looked at peace and frequently smiled, but occasionally David would catch her staring into space and the ghost would return. It was dark and ominous. It looked like death.

Then just as suddenly as she had arrived, four days after he had met her at Blooming Foods, David woke up to find the sleeping bag and pad rolled up with a note that simply said, "Thank you for your kindness. Flower." She was gone. He crumpled the note, and after a few moments began to cry. He felt like he had failed her. For a few days, he hoped for her to return and drove around Bloomington and the surrounding area searching for her. Eventually he gave up, admitting to himself she was really gone.

David would never see Flower again, but he did make a vow. He would use Sycamore Hill to reach out to people like her and give them a glimpse of the beauty and the peace that had put a smile on her face, the beauty and peace that had saved his life. He would do his best to help them on their journeys, wherever they were headed, and he would get better at talking to them and helping them process the demons, and the devils, and the fears that haunted their souls. And for the rest of his life, every day, he would pray for Flower, on his knees, right next to where she had planted her red tulip.

Chapter 11:

Launch

Jason and Zoe were loading Jason's van. It was almost ready for the journey and the adventure that lay ahead. In the back where he had removed the standard bench seats were a bed, a table, a chair, plenty of storage, a Coleman gas stove and lantern, and space for all of your standard camping supplies – tent, sleeping bag, sleeping pad, back pack, etc. He was equipped for almost any adventure he might happen upon. Zoe had even bought a sticker that she placed on the back of the van that proudly stated, "Not all who wander are lost."

Jason and Zoe carefully loaded clothes, books, dry food, Coleman fuel, and other staples he would need for the road. Even though this meant that they would soon be parting ways, there was joy. They felt as if their lives were beginning again, a new start that they felt blessed to be sharing with each other. And just below the surface, the love they both knew was waiting to bloom, but not just yet.

"Looks like you are about ready," Zoe observed as the last of Jason's bags were loaded into the van.

"I think so. Been thinking about this for so long I can't believe the day is finally here." Jason threw the bag he was holding into the back of the van and shut the door. "I'm ready. Still not even sure where I'll stop and sleep tonight, or when I'll stop driving."

"That sounds like a good place to be," Zoe said with a hint of envy.

"How about you, Zoe, what's next?" Jason asked. "You said you were going to stay in Bloomington for a while."

"I have a few things I need to finish here. I only have a year left in school. I was majoring in zoology, and I think I might also take some French classes. You never know though, I'll see how the year goes. Maybe it's not about what I finish, but where this all leads. We'll see." She twirled around and continued, "Who knows? Maybe when I'm done I'll move somewhere by the ocean and try to work with animals, maybe dolphins."

"You could build your own paradise." Jason envisioned the tropical paradise Zoe might create. No doubt with its own espresso bar!

"I don't know about a tropical paradise," she corrected Jason, "but wherever it is, it will be one hundred percent Zoe! My own personal Sycamore Hill," awakening to possibilities, her mind envisioned a myriad of potential destinations. As attractive as they all were, she still had her eyes set on something much closer. "If anything, I'm much more excited about being able to visit David over the next year than I am about finishing up my degree. Of course, it'll be good to finish something. I feel like I've been running my entire life."

"I know what you mean," Jason affirmed. "Ever since I got back from Iraq it's like I've been a rat in a cage.

Even though I'll be on the road, it feels like my head is finally slowing down and I will be able to live again."

"What do you think about how David keeps talking about spiritual things as if they are real and the answer to everything?" Zoe asked. David had been pulling on her "spirit" strings and she wanted to make sure she wasn't the only one.

"I'm not totally sure," Jason admitted, "but I do know I feel something when I'm with David, and the last couple nights when I went to bed I actually prayed and it didn't feel stupid. In a weird way, I think there just might be a reason to all of this, and I guess more than anything that helps me believe there just might be a God, or at least something bigger than us who is behind all of this."

"Me, too, although I never thought I would believe it." Zoe looked up in the sky then back at Jason. Only a few days earlier she would have mocked the idea of God. Today was a new day. "The idea – God wants us to draw near to him – makes sense to me. I just don't know if I will ever make peace with all of the abuse I've suffered. I want to believe God understands the pain, I can take comfort in that." She stopped to consider that for a moment then continued, "I can believe that cry on the cross, the forsaken cry David talked to us about. The strange thing is that when I'm able to believe it, all of a sudden the idea of – rising from the grave – makes sense too. But then the next moment I don't believe and it doesn't make so much sense. I'm trying hard to hold on to the believe part."

"Yeah, I guess I can just say I believe," Jason said softly and then with more assurance, "Now I just have to figure out what 'believe' means."

"I bet David would say it means to keep moving forward, keep drawing closer, keep falling down on your knees," Zoe guessed accurately.

"The knees part won't be hard!" Jason smiled and exclaimed. "Lord knows I've been there plenty of times!"

"Can I ask you something, Zoe?" Jason shifted gears, becoming serious.

"Sure, although from the look on your face it must be heavy," she answered with a hint of trepidation in her eyes. The closer they got to one another the more she felt the urgency of attraction. But this question wasn't about love.

"Well, I was just wondering," Jason said about as shyly as a former Marine could ever be, "why did you trust me that day we met? It's pretty obvious from our talks at David's that you haven't trusted men in a long time, yet you trusted me, almost instantly. Why?" genuinely curious, he also half way hoped it was because she had been instantly smitten with him. He was in for a shock.

Zoe hesitated for a second, but she had known this revelation would have to come eventually and she was prepared. She answered.

"You know the other day when you were talking about killing, and that man in Indianapolis?"

"Yes."

"Well, I already knew about it," Zoe revealed.

"You did?" Jason processed the revelation for a moment, and then continued. "Why didn't you say something?" Jason was confused. *She had known?*

"Well, it's not easy to talk about, and meeting you was hard to imagine, much less believe it was actually happening. You see, that man you killed is the man who raped me when I was 13," she answered and then looked away. It was a stunning coincidence to process. Could a rape and a killing be the fate that set their paths on a course for each other? That was crazy.

Jason didn't reply immediately; he had to let the weight of what Zoe had just said sink in. When it did, he wasn't sure how to respond. "Oh, Zoe. I don't even know what to say." Without thinking, he put his arms around her and they hugged tightly, urgently.

"You don't have to say anything," she whispered in his ear. And she meant it, being there together and holding each other was enough. "It's all so weird. Think about it. If not for that evil man we would have never met and would have never found our way to David," she finished and held Jason tighter.

After what was either a minute or an hour, it was hard to tell, they separated and tried to make sense of it. Jason sat down on the curb next to the van and Zoe joined him. There was much to consider.

"Talk about fate," Jason said with a subtle astonishment, "what are the odds of that?"

"Not great," Zoe stated the obvious. "Yet, I can't believe I was raped on purpose for some sort of destiny. That's just too much to believe, but here we are, and I'm ready to live again, for the first time in my life. I mean, I can't imagine life without all that I've learned in just a few days." It was incredibly hard for Zoe to process what this all meant in light of where she had been. Luckily, she was overcome by the thankfulness of the moment rather than the pain of the past.

"Yeah, I don't think David would say that what happened to you pre-ordained this or pre-destined this," Jason hypothesized. "I think he'd say we both have used horrible things to draw closer to God, and when you do that, amazing things can happen, even miraculous. And this is all that matters."

"Yes, it is," Zoe agreed, "cause and effect can get confusing real fast. I guess that is why I am ready to finish up here in Bloomington. I want to learn to focus on the moment, what is right in front of me. I'm tired of regret holding me back."

"I hope I find what I need on this trip, although I'm not so sure it's what I find but how I go about looking for it," Jason explained. "My goal is to make each day its own story, its own destination."

"I think that is what David means by walking toward God," Zoe added. "It's being in the moment, allowing ourselves the wonder of living like we were really created for a purpose. The second I stepped foot on Sycamore Hill I felt hope, and now I'm beginning to feel alive. Maybe for the first time in my life. And what's even stranger, considering where I've been, I've been praying. I can't stop."

"What have you been praying for?" Jason asked.

"Praying for? Nothing really. Really just being mindful of God and giving thanks for not killing myself and the opportunity I now have to live. My praying is really just following," Zoe summed up her spiritual journey at Sycamore Hill.

"That sounds like a good place to be, Zoe," Jason said, happy for her. "Maybe I'll find some of those same prayers on the road. I think it will be easier for me to believe than to pray. Of course, knowing I killed the punk who brutalized you, it would be hard not to believe." He turned toward Zoe and smiled, he wanted to kiss her, but he settled for a hug.

"I'll be praying for you," she assured Jason as they separated from the hug. As the words left her mouth, Zoe couldn't believe it. She'd said she'd be praying for somebody! Yet, it felt so real, so natural. And then she added commentary that seemed to have popped straight into her head from David's mouth. "And remember, if I've learned anything from David, it's that real belief comes from true prayer." Then she added with a wink, "The kind you find down on your knees."

"There is no doubt about that," Jason replied with resolve. Something powerful had brought them together and both of them to David, and it was a force he couldn't deny.

As much as they would have loved to continue talking and ponder the complexity and wonder of their journey towards each other, the van was ready to go and Jason's journey needed to begin. But first, it was time for one last visit to Sycamore Hill. Zoe and Jason both wanted to say goodbye, and although neither had admitted it to the other, they were both hoping for some sort of blessing or words of wisdom from David. They had come to Sycamore Hill lost, now they had found the fire of life. If they had known the words to the old hymn, "Amazing Grace," they would have started singing.

"Well, I think I'm ready," Jason acknowledged looking at the loaded up and buttoned down van. "Let's go over to David's so I can say goodbye."

"Good idea," Zoe agreed, rising from the curb to open the door to the passenger side of the van so she could get in. Jason joined her, turned the ignition, and soon they were parking in the familiar spot at the foot of Sycamore Hill.

Chapter 12:

Lord Have Mercy

Their feet were light, but their hearts were a bit heavy as Jason and Zoe made their way up the path to Sycamore Hill. Both were excited about the journey unfolding in front of them, but they were also a bit melancholy that this would probably be the last time in a while, if ever again, that they would be together with David on Sycamore Hill. As the clearing came into view there was David, as if he had been waiting for them, on his porch drinking tea. It was an image that they would forever take with them.

"Hey guys!" David yelled as they walked across the clearing. "Glad you could come by before Jason left."

"I wouldn't leave without one last goodbye," Jason assured David.

"Come up here and let's have one last drink," David invited them.

Jason and Zoe walked up on the porch and took a seat where David handed them both a big glass of tea from the pitcher sitting next to him. They took a seat and looked out across the garden. It was early summer and colors were alive everywhere.

"So where are you going first, Jason?" David asked taking a big swig.

"Well, I'm heading west, but I think I'm going to take the long way," Jason said as if he had all the time in the world. "I have always wanted to see Michigan's Upper Peninsula, so I'm heading there first."

"I love the Upper Peninsula," David shared. "My family and I used to go to Mackinaw Island."

"Isn't that the island where they don't allow cars?" Zoe recognized the name.

"That's the place," David affirmed. "It's like stepping back to the 1800s. If you can get away from the tourists, the quiet there is similar to what I have here at Sycamore Hill. Sometimes when I am just lying in the grass listening to the sounds of nature, I am transported back to Mackinaw and time spent there with Mary and the kids. Those are always good memories."

"You must miss them a lot," Zoe said empathetically.

"I do," David paused, "but I was serious about what I said before. When I'm alone out here and everything is still, I often just stop and pray. I can feel so close to them it is like I am with them in heaven. It is no dream, it is something real – a space that allows me to embrace the good memories without regret, even when regret is doing its best to overwhelm me."

"I believe you," Zoe followed. "Even though Jason is leaving and I'm not sure of much beyond finishing school, somehow I know that you all will never be far from me. Regardless of where we are."

"I know," Jason added. "I almost feel like I'm taking you both with me on this trip."

"You are right," David leaned closer to them. "When we are living, especially when we are in relationships with others, life feels connected, even when we are alone. But beware; the moment we leave situations like this, all that would divide and isolate us can come suddenly and without warning. Life is a continual battle to focus on true meaning and purpose." David reached into his pocket and grabbed what looked like two short black cloth necklaces. "Here, I made these for you two. They are prayer ropes." Each was about 18 inches long and made out of black yarn, knitted with knots, and sewn into the middle of each was a small wooden cross.

"Prayer ropes?" Jason queried. As much as he had begun to believe in God, he had never once in his life thought he'd be carrying a prayer rope.

"Yes, prayer ropes. Don't worry about what to say. Just keep them in your pocket as a reminder to pray, wherever you are," David instructed. "It can be simple. If I don't have something to say in particular at the moment, I'll just repeat, 'Lord Jesus Christ have mercy on me a sinner,' or even simpler, 'Lord have mercy.' It's an ancient prayer and will help keep you focused on God and living in this moment."

"That is simple enough," Zoe agreed and then grinned. "I can't promise how often I will actually pray, but I will keep it with me." But she was being funny; she knew immediately she would use it. In fact, she would wear it out and someday receive another from David.

"I like that, simple," Jason followed. "I can do that. Lord knows I'll have plenty of time to practice on the road."

"And whatever happens, always come back to that, prayer, on your knees if possible," David counseled them. "The worst of life might be over, or the worst might be yet to come, but whatever happens, remember that you are never truly alone. You can always use your pain as a reminder by contemplating how far you've come and by helping another struggling with the same darkness, even a stranger. Draw closer to God and you begin to draw strength from the one who created it all."

"I'll do my best," Jason assured David and Zoe nodded in agreement. "So what about you?" Jason wondered. "What does the future hold for David?"

"More of the same probably," David smiled. "This is my home, and I have much more work to do. For now, I will keep building, keep planting, keep talking to my new friends." He took another swig of tea and stated with a shining face, "Sycamore Hill is so full of life, I can't really imagine ever leaving."

Jason finished his drink and rose. As much as he hated to leave Sycamore Hill, he was anxious to get on the road. If this went on any longer it would just get harder to leave. Zoe followed his lead and they both walked forward to give David a big hug and say goodbye.

"Safe travels, my friend," David said to Jason. Then he looked over at Zoe, "And I hope to see you again soon."

"You will," Zoe answered.

"I'll be safe, except when it's fun not to be safe," Jason followed with a mischievous grin. There would be prayer on the trip, but also fun.

And then, as suddenly as that first meeting with David back at Blooming Foods, they were back in the van, and the journey was about to begin. Just a few days earlier they had been strangers on a collision course with darkness, the forever kind of darkness. Now there was light and friendship. There was hope and purpose. While apart, in spirit they would still be together and because of that they would not be alone.

Chapter 13:

Goodbyes and Beginnings

As they pulled away from Sycamore Hill, Jason's van was quiet. Jason and Zoe were excited and grateful for their short time together, but there was about to be a goodbye, and goodbyes were always a little sad. For each of them, what seemed like a lifetime of pain had been processed in a few, fantastic days and it left them a bit soul-tired. After hours of talking and listening, it was time to act. For Jason that meant setting out on his adventure, for Zoe, school and work, finishing what she had started and continuing to visit David when needed. Neither was thinking much past that immediate future, but both knew this wouldn't be the last time they'd be together. The fellowship they had discovered with each other and David was too deep for that. Really, it was love, a deeper love than either had ever felt before. It was this love that made it hard to say goodbye. So, despite being determined to continue their paths separately for a season, Jason suggested they stop by the Runciple Spoon for one last Dirty Hippie.

"How about we go by the Spoon one last time?" Jason asked.

"The Spoon, I don't know. How about we try something new. A friend of mine works at Le Petit Café'. Let's do a little French," Zoe suggested and Jason agreed.

"That's a great idea. I'll imagine we are having a cappuccino in Paris," Jason smiled at the thought.

They sat in the back corner of Le Petit Café', a cozy, neighborhood French café, where they nursed cappuccinos and shared a French cherry pastry, taking time to relish the moment. He couldn't help but look at Zoe and see what he could only describe as his angel. They had begun to find salvation together and she glimmered.

"It's amazing," Jason shared. "To think how close we've been to Sycamore Hill and David, and to each other all these years. I would never have thought that just a few miles from Bloomington were the answers I needed, in a place so simple. I mean, he lives completely old school."

"He sure does," Zoe agreed. "His old school sure is good though. It was eye opening to not see any sign of cell phones and computers, yet still feel so incredibly alive. I think half the reason I didn't say much at first was that it was hard to believe it was real. I kept waiting for David to turn into some kind of freak or worse!" She laughed. "It's a good thing I knew I could trust him."

"Well, he's far from a freak," Jason joined her laughter and tried to imagine David as some hippie freak guru. "He's probably the most clear-headed, real human being I've ever met. Just sitting there with him, talking, made life seem like it should always be like that."

"We make it complicated. Don't we?" Zoe asked.

"We sure do. Complicated with crap that has little to do with living, and much to do with distracting us from the fact that we are not living," Jason wryly observed. He'd been listening to David and becoming more aware of what living meant.

"That's really the point, isn't it, to live," Zoe stated and took a sip of her cappuccino.

"Yes, but that also means understanding that our life was meant to be led by purpose, and the closer we draw to God, the easier it is to find the purpose and stay focused in it," Jason contemplated. "Life without meaning is hell. Life with meaning ultimately leads to God and that is heaven. It is real." Jason wasn't concerned with being theologically accurate; he just knew he needed to keep following God, and that got him more excited for his journey than anything. If he was following God, he was sure it would lead to amazing things, and more importantly, back to Zoe.

"I've had enough of hell," Zoe observed, laughter replaced by serious reflection.

"Me too," Jason agreed as they both finished their drinks and pastry. They lingered, but it was time to leave.

"I guess we better be going," Jason suggested, staring at his empty coffee cup.

"It's time," was Zoe's short reply. She knew they couldn't put this off any longer. Life couldn't move forward, until they moved forward.

They walked out of the café. Soon Jason would be dropping off Zoe and his road adventure would begin. He was excited, but sad. He would miss David and Sycamore Hill. He would really miss Zoe. He loved her and wanted to tell her, but the road was calling and he knew it wasn't the time to profess his love, or was it?

After the short drive from the café, they pulled up to Zoe's apartment and it was finally time for goodbyes.

"Well, I guess this is where we say goodbye," Jason stated slowly, "for now at least."

"Stay in touch and keep me updated. Send an e-mail when you get a chance," Zoe invited him. Saying the word e-mail shocked them both. From the moment they met and had joined David at Sycamore Hill they had been almost technology free. And the reality was that even an e-mail might be a while. Jason was only bringing a simple pre-paid phone, and since he planned on staying as much off the beaten path as possible, he would effectively be off the grid. As hard as that would be, he was looking forward to the isolation, especially after experiencing the clean air and clear headedness of Sycamore Hill. He was tired of being connected. Surfing the web offered too many opportunities for viewing the triggers that brought him back to Iraq, and too many distractions from living that encouraged bad habits. The simple life at Sycamore Hill had been better for him and he planned on trying to continue it on his trip.

"I will. I promise to give you updates anytime something noteworthy happens, or I just miss you," Jason winked.

"You'll miss me," Zoe smiled back. They both knew it was true. More than anything else they had experienced together, they would miss each other's company deeply. It was a heavy moment with a swirling soup of emotions in the air. While Zoe had come a long way since first meeting Jason and learning to heal at Sycamore Hill, it was time to let go and let Jason continue on his trip. A long goodbye would just be more painful.

"Now you need to get going. You still have plenty of time to go a long way today. And we need to stop before I cry." Although Zoe wasn't crying yet, she meant it.

"Alright then, I guess it's time," Jason answered and stepped into the van where he closed the door and Zoe approached for goodbye.

"You be careful, and never be afraid to chase whatever you may find out there," Zoe encouraged him.

"You bet," he reached out and gave her a playful tap on the head. "You've come a long way, Zoe. I hope you are able to learn more from David." Jason would miss David and his wisdom on the trip. He was glad he had the prayer rope.

"I know. I have much more to learn from him. Since I've actually begun praying, hopefully someone is listening." Zoe smiled. She was determined to hold on to the faith building inside her.

Jason turned the ignition of the van, put the transmission into drive, and turned toward Zoe as he held on the brake waiting to leave. He wanted to tell her *come with me, I love you*. But goodbye was all he could manage. "Goodbye, Zoe, I'll miss you. Look for an e-mail sooner than later."

"Be safe, Jason," Zoe answered simply and Jason began to pull away. As he did, Zoe waved and under her breath whispered to herself, "I should just jump in that van with him." Jason couldn't tell what she was saying or hear her, but as he pulled away from the curb and looked at Zoe through the rear view mirror, the only feeling he had for her was love. Real, deep, pure love. He knew he would see her again.

Chapter 14:

Alone, but Not Alone

Zoe was studying in the Herman B Wells library on the campus of Indiana University. It had been almost a month since Jason had left for his trip and she was back in school, working hard to finish her zoology degree. Her main focus though wasn't zoology; it was the French class she was taking in earnest. The more she learned the more comfortable she became with the idea of being an au pair in the French wine country. It might not be such a bad idea after all, or maybe something else. The more she was able to get back into the swing of the life, the more she was able to embrace life's many possibilities. There was really no telling where this year of study would lead.

Jason and she had exchanged a few long e-mails the last few weeks, but he was almost completely off the grid out west and they had been sporadic. Jason stopped at a library to use their Internet when he could, but that was okay. It wasn't always easy getting back into the rhythm of school, and if they had been constantly messaging it would have been a distraction for Zoe. She had been to Sycamore Hill a couple of times already. It was mainly just to help David with the grounds, and they talked little except when taking a break. That was fine with Zoe; she was more than happy for the escape from Bloomington and the hard physical work at Sycamore Hill. The effort always seemed to cleanse her mind and leave her with hope and energy for the moment and whatever was to come.

Hidden in a back corner of the library near the zoology section, she was having a hard time focusing. The hardest parts of school were the late night walks back from the library and her one evening class. Walks in the dark had always been tough, ever since the attack. A large campus like Bloomington held many dark corridors and hidden doorways at night where her imagination could picture lurkers in waiting. She was ready to walk home now, but as usual, it felt much safer to continue sitting in the safety of the library. But the longer she sat, the later she would get home, and the later she got home, the more likely it was she would sit alone in the dark of her room. Alone in the dark, the demons might come. While she had come a long way since meeting David and Jason, the demons still lurked in the shadows.

But Zoe wasn't hopeless. She was becoming more hopeful, increasingly brave. Sycamore Hill and the friendship with David and Jason had armed her. She reached into her purse and took out the prayer rope that David had given her. Leaning forward she began to pray softly under her lips, "Lord have mercy. Lord have mercy. Lord have mercy." She pictured Jason in the middle of a majestic western vista and his happiness made her happy. Her mind wandered back to Sycamore Hill where David's smile greeted her. She continued to pray and after a few minutes felt warm. She believed it was God. The darkness was becoming light and she was getting better and better at learning to move forward and live.

She was not alone.

Jason was somewhere in the middle of Wyoming, the tenth largest but least populated of the United States. To be alone in Wyoming was to be truly alone. He had driven late into the night on a two-lane state highway where he had not see another soul for almost an hour. Staring into the darkness he noticed that wherever he looked there were no lights, not even a rancher's beacon to be seen on the horizon. It was nothing but darkness and stars. He pulled his van over to the curb and stopped.

He remembered a friend who had told him that in the remotest parts of the United States, far from lights and civilization, the night sky blew up with stars. Seeing no artificial light other than what was being given off from the van he remembered his friend's description and decided to stop and have a look up. It was as remote a place as he had been since his trip began a few weeks earlier.

Stepping out of the van, he closed his eyelids for a minute to lose the residue of the van's interior and the headlights and retain full use of his night vision. Opening them he looked up, and his mouth dropped open. The sky exploded. The Milky Way expanded in every direction like pictures he had seen in schoolbooks, pictures he thought could only be observed from a telescope orbiting in outer space.

He moved further from the side of the road and fell to his knees in the prairie grass, his head still looking up. He was in awe. The sky was a black canvas covered in shimmering stars of all sizes. He wished they were with him. He dreamt of Zoe being there and the two of them lying there under the stars on a sleeping bag until they fell asleep. Oh, the adventures they would have. And David. This was the peace of Sycamore Hill on heavenly steroids. Jason wished he could be here, too, to see all the wonder. There were shooting stars and the celestial lights above were so close it seemed as if he could climb on a nearby ridge and touch them.

He reached into his coat pocket and pulled out the prayer rope he had been given by David. Still looking up, he began to pray, "Lord Jesus Christ, have mercy on me a sinner." He preferred the longer version of the prayer David had suggested. After a few minutes, he began talking to God out loud, giving thanks for the chance to live again, thanks for having met Zoe and David, and thanks for the stars above his head. Overcome by it all, he began to cry. Not sad tears, but joyful tears. And he knew he was not alone.

David had woken just before sunrise and after doing a few chores percolated some coffee. He filled a mug with piping hot java and then walked outside where he sat down on a chair near the main flowerbed of his front yard, more specifically, in front of Flower's red tulip, and began to read his Bible under the warm glow of the rising sun. He opened the yellowed and worn pages to the Psalms and began to read from his favorite, the 40th Psalm:

> *I waited patiently for the Lord; and he inclined to me, and heard my cry. He brought me up also out of a horrible pit, out of the miry clay, and set my feet upon a rock, and established my goings. And he hath put a new song in my mouth, even praise unto our God: many shall see it, and fear, and shall trust in the Lord.*

David believed and David trusted. He had been through hell and delivered to a place called Sycamore Hill where he had brought hope to the hopeless for 30 years. He was grateful. Yet, there was still despair. As he continued to read from the Psalms, the words began to ring hollow. He couldn't help but focus on Flower's red tulip and wonder if she had found salvation or death at the hands of some brutalizer, or from a dirty needle stuck in her vein. He had wondered hundreds of times in the years since she left. He began to cry as the face of Flower in his mind morphed into that of his family. He began to feel alone. Deathly alone. It was a desperate feeling. He put down the Bible and pulled the well-worn prayer rope from his back pocket and collapsed to the ground that was still covered in dew. As he ran the prayer rope through his fingers, his mind began to cry out to God. Why? Why? Why? It was always why? And, where are you? He would pray until it subsided, or he stopped crying. Sometimes, it was other things that interrupted these moments of darkness.

David had been living at Sycamore Hill for decades and was as much a part of the forest as the forest was a part of him. This communion with nature could bridge the gap of despair he felt at times like this and reconnect him with the peace of God, the Creator. As he calmed himself with prayer, he heard a rustling in the woods and looked up. It was a young deer, the fawn of an old friend who had been running through his forest for years. David sat up and reached into the bag he always had with him on these mornings. It was full of grain and he grabbed a handful and held out his hand. The fawn approached and as she ate from the palm of his right hand, he stroked her head with his left. He was able to smile and was reminded just how blessed life was on Sycamore Hill. He thought of all the people who had visited. People like Jason, Zoe, Flower, and the many others. Tears ran down his face, but he was happy. Life was full of wonder, peace and pain, love and suffering, grace and the small miracles we find when we allow ourselves to walk with God. Miracles found on our knees, claiming forgiveness through the power of humility when we stopped fighting and began to listen. They are found when we serve others and use our heartbreak as fuel to comfort those without comfort. They are found when we allow ourselves to let God feel the pain of our suffering, because he understands. David had learned all of this, and he was teaching it to whomever came to him, and to whomever he found in need. Because of this, in spite of his guilt and pain and regret, David was not alone.

And neither are you.

Author Bio:

Silouan Green is a speaker and writer. He survived a tragic jet crash to overcome severe PTSD thanks to an epic two-year motorcycle journey, and now helps others find healing and purpose.

Sycamore Hill is his third published book and he has spoken to over 500 groups and organizations around the United States on PTSD, Moral Injury, Music Therapy, Peer Support, and Resiliency. He is the creator of The Ladder UPP, a life skills program for anyone needing accountability and direction in their life.

Silouan lives in the woods with his wife and eight children on their own Sycamore Hill.